RATIONALITIES OF PLANNING

Rationalities of Planning

Development versus environment in planning for housing

JONATHAN MURDOCH
Department of City and Regional Planning
Cardiff University, UK

SIMONE ABRAM
Department of Town and Regional Planning
University of Sheffield, UK

Ashgate

Published by
Ashgate Publishing Limited
Gower House
Croft Road
Aldershot
Hampshire GU11 3HR
England

Ashgate Publishing Company
131 Main Street
Burlington, VT 05401-5600 USA

Ashgate website: http://www.ashgate.com

British Library Cataloguing in Publication Data
Murdoch, Jonathan
        Rationalities of planning : development versus environment
        in planning for housing
        1. Housing - England
        I. Title II. Abram, Simone
        363.5'0942

Library of Congress Control Number: 2001096372

ISBN 1 84014 929 9

Printed and bound in Great Britain by
Antony Rowe Ltd, Chippenham, Wiltshire

Contents

List of Figures		*vi*
List of Tables		*vii*
List of Photographs		*viii*
Acknowledgements		*ix*
List of Abbreviations		*x*

1. Planning and the Governance of Growth: Theories and Issues   1

2. The Changing Rationalities of Planning Policy   17

3. The Policy Hierarchy in Planning   43

4. Planning by Numbers   65

5. Competing Rationalities in Structure Planning   83

6. Down to the District: Local Expressions of Development and Environment   111

7. Towards a New Rationality of Planning?   133

Bibliography   *149*
Index   *159*

List of Figures

Figure 5.1   Map of the Buckinghamshire study area   85

Figure 5.2   Arrangements at the Buckinghamshire EiP   100

Figure 6.1   Housing sites in Haddenham   123

List of Tables

Table 2.1   Population change for largely rural districts   35

Table 2.2   Net migration change in English counties   35

Table 5.1   Economic activity in the south east   86

Table 5.2   Average weekly earnings in the south east   87

List of Photographs

Plate 5.1   Buckinghamshire County Hall, Aylesbury,   90
             and County Library approach

Plate 6.1   Aylesbury's market square, with the 1970s   113
             County Hall and 1980s shopping centre in
             the background

Plate 6.2   Haddenham 'Church End'   120

Acknowledgements

We are would like to thank the Economic and Social Research Council for sponsoring the two research projects - *Exclusive Space: networks of participation and forward planning*, as part of the Local Governance Initiative (1994-1995), and *Planning as Metaphor: mediating aspirations for community and environment* (1996-1997) - which are reported in this book. We would also like to acknowledge the assistance of Terry Marsden who worked with us on the first of these projects. Most gratitude, however, must be extended to the research respondents in Buckinghamshire who gave so generously of their time, knowledge and hospitality. These respondents include planners at Buckinghamshire County Council and Aylesbury Vale District Council, participants in the Buckinghamshire Structure Plan review process, and the people of Haddenham. We would like to extend particular thanks to Chris Kennenford and Doug Bamsey who, on a number of occasions, answered our many (tiresome) questions with great patience. Our thanks are also due for the hospitality of the Buckinghamshire County and Aylesbury District councillors who accepted our presence at numerous meetings, and gave generously of their time in response to our requests. We should also particularly like to thank Renee and Mick Maguire for their unfailing generosity and friendship, and our friends in the Haddenham Village Society, the Protection Society, the Parish Council, the Haddenham Badminton Club and the many other villagers who made this study possible.

List of Abbreviations

AAL	Area of Attractive Landscape
AONB	Area of Outstanding Natural Beauty
AVDC	Aylesbury Vale District Council
BCC	Buckinghamshire County Council
CPRE	Council for the Protection of Rural England
DETR	Department of the Environment, Transport and the Regions
DLP	District Local Plan
DoE	Department of the Environment (pre-1997)
EiP	Examination-in-Public
GOR	Government Offices for the Regions
GOSE	Government Office for the South East
HBF	House Builders Federation
HPS	Haddenham Protection Society
HVS	Haddenham Village Society
MAFF	Ministry for Agriculture, Forestry and Fisheries
MPG	Minerals Policy Guidance
NGO	Non-Governmental Organization
NIMBY	Not In My Back Yard
PPG	Planning Policy Guidance
QUANGO	Quasi Autonomous Non-Governmental Organization
RDA	Regional Development Agency
ROSE	Rest of the South East
RPB	Regional Planning Body
RPC	Regional Planning Conference
RPG	Regional Planning Guidance
RTPI	Royal Town Planning Institute
SERPLAN	South East Regional Planning Forum
TCPA	Town and Country Planning Association
TEC	Training and Enterprise Council
TVCCI	Thames Valley Chamber of Commerce and Industry
UDP	Unitary Development Plan

Chapter 1

Planning and the Governance of Growth: Theories and Issues

Introduction

Access to a dwelling, to a place to live, is a fundamental human need. For this reason, housing is a 'public good', one which should be available to all. Yet, in England in recent times, housing has become a source of great conflict: instead of being perceived as a 'good', for many it is a form of 'pollution', one that emerges in the shape of unsightly 'blots' on the landscape. A profound ambivalence about housing has thus embedded itself in many areas of political and social life, so that the assumed benefits of housing provision have come to be challenged. One consequence of this challenge may ultimately be shortages of housing for those citizens that need them most.

In part, ambivalence around the meaning and status of housing can be seen as the inevitable consequence of the UK's population density (which stands at 241 people per square kilometre, compared with 30 in the US and 107 in France) leading to growing numbers of households competing ever more fiercely over a diminishing land resource. Clearly, the pressure for new housing that stems from higher numbers of (smaller) households on these rather cramped islands is a key factor in explaining changing perceptions of housing and house building. It should be noted, however, that conflicts around housing land are most intense not in areas which already contain large numbers of houses - e.g. *urban* areas - but in places where there are the least numbers of new houses - e.g. *rural* areas. Housing development is especially unwelcome in the most 'environmentally rich' locations; yet, these locations are the ones where demand for houses is highest.

The use of the countryside for new houses frequently provokes an outcry amongst existing rural residents (Short *et al.*, 1986). Rural dwellers often perceive housing developers as insatiable consumers of the rural environment or, alternatively, as agents promoting a creeping suburbanisation of the countryside. They feel the incursion of new housing will inevitably lead to the destruction of rural environments and communities. The development of new housing is, therefore, something to be resisted, for it seems to violate the settled and tranquil nature of the rural realm (Matless, 1995). Newspapers now regularly feature stories about local action groups and their campaigns against new housing development. To take just one example, *The Guardian* on February 16th 1998 carried an article

1

which proclaimed that 'the barricade is up on Acacia Drive. Behind it are the builders with plans to put up 92 houses in a field. On the other side, the normally peaceful villagers are angry. Very angry'. In this case, the local council had granted permission for the construction of 82 detached houses and 10 'affordable' homes on a piece of green land on the edge of a village. The local residents responded by forming an action group - Residents Action Group for the Environment (RAGE) - and tried to occupy the field before the builders could begin construction. The developer gained a court order to remove the villagers and then put up a fence to keep all residents off the site, with security guards employed to restrict access. Thus, the villagers found themselves hemmed in by security measures, introduced in order to facilitate the building of new houses (and, of course, to bring in more villagers who would quite possibly, in turn, resist any further development). As this example indicates, the fight against housing can often be traumatic for rural communities and it can severely undermine the harmony and tranquillity that is often thought to distinguish life in the countryside.

Conflict of this type is now quite usual in rural areas. In many regions of the UK, the pressure for new housing runs up against profound concerns about environmental degradation, the loss of land to development, and the relentless expansion of towns and villages. This conflict is most evident in the south of England where the pressure for new homes is intense (especially in the 'well-heeled' shire counties to the south, west and north of London). The demands on rural land for housing have emerged because of a drift of population nationally from north to south and a simultaneous movement of households away from the cities. It has therefore been calculated that the population of the south-east region - which is already home to 18 million people – will continue to grow, but most importantly this growth will be concentrated in the areas *outside* London. Government statisticians propose that a further 1.1 million households will form in the region (excluding London) in the years up to 2016 (DETR, 1999a). The scope for conflict over rural housing is clearly exacerbated by these trends.

In this book we wish to investigate the friction between the provision of housing and the protection of rural land as it is experienced in the English context. In particular, we are interested in how the two views of housing - on the one hand, a 'public good', on the other hand, 'pollution' - come to be asserted in the planning arena. The planning system is responsible for 'governing growth' in that it has to ensure development takes place which meets the country's economic and social needs. However, planning is also encouraged to ensure that this development somehow respects the natural environment. Thus, planning authorities are required to achieve a 'balancing act' between development and environmental protection: they must guarantee, in the current jargon, that development is 'sustainable'. Planners, moreover, have to maintain this balancing act while also involving the general public in planning decisions. Thus, when local authorities draw up the development plans that specify how particular geographical areas are to be developed over given time periods, local residents are invited to comment on the proposals. These comments are - in theory, at least - used to shape the final outcome in terms of plan policies. The general public is also permitted to comment on specific development proposals as they come forward, and again these comments may have some bearing on the final decisions taken.

It is not only the general public that becomes involved in plan making and development control decisions: economic and environmental interests also seek to influence planning in the course of public consultation exercises. For developers it is important that planning policies take account of the need for development and they seek to ensure that development opportunities are opened up in development plans. For environmentalists it is important that plan policies pay due heed to local natural conditions and (often in alliance with local residents) they seek to ensure that as much environmental protection as possible is enshrined in plans. As a consequence, the reviews of plans can be overshadowed by heated disputes between the various protagonists, to the extent that planners often find themselves struggling to adjudicate between the irreconcilable differences in the views of those they are meant to consider.

We characterize the debate that follows from the participation of various interests in planning processes as a contest between discourses of 'development' and 'environment'. In this respect, we use the term 'discourse' loosely: it simply refers to all the various arguments and actions that lie behind a certain set of goals. In the context of planning for housing, we can see, on the one hand, a whole range of interests, programmes, policies and proposals that seek to assert a *developmental* agenda while, on the other hand, there are a number of actors and interests that push an *environmentalist* or *protectionist* agenda. On one side of the argument there will typically be groups such as the House Builders Federation (HBF) along with other developer representatives (such as planning consultants), while on the other side we find environmental groups, such as the Council for the Protection of Rural England (CPRE) - which, as its name suggests, wishes to protect rural land from extensive new housing developments - and rural residents who are concerned at the seemingly endless demands on the countryside. These groups use the planning system in order to pursue widely differing goals.

Planning is constantly seeking to assess the merits of development against the demands of conservation. However, in making such assessments it is not neutral: it has its own goals, policies and modes of operation. In Chapter 2, we outline the main thrust of planning policy by examining how the two discourses of 'development' and 'environment' have been framed by government. During the 1980s, the system was streamlined by Mrs Thatcher's Conservative governments in the hope that it could become more responsive to the market, thereby emphasizing the system's inherent 'developmentalism'. However, in response to a groundswell of opposition that emerged against this more market-led approach, a gradual strengthening of planning took place so that by the end of the 1990s environmental protection was once again a key concern. At the present time, the balance between developmental and environmental considerations is to be achieved through the pursuit of 'sustainable development'. This concept has emerged as a seemingly vital means of reconciling developmental and environmental concerns. In turn, the shift to sustainability has been bolstered by increased public participation, notably on the part of social actors concerned with protection of the countryside. We describe moves to open up the planning system to participation and the way these moves are likely to facilitate increased rural protection.

Local planning policy is not only shaped by the contest between discourses of development and environment: it is also configured by the tiers of government and their complex interrelations. In Chapter 3, we consider the governmental hierarchy in planning and ask whether policy emerges from a governmental system of loosely interlocked tiers, in which each tier has discretion to act in autonomous ways, or whether planning is determined by a top-down system of central state direction. This issue is important because the structure of government can either impose a singular policy 'line' or can facilitate the development of locally-tailored strategies. We show that, in important respects, the state does both these things simultaneously, leading to a number of tensions running through planning policy.

Nowhere are these tensions more evident than in the housing arena, which is considered in some detail in Chapter 4. In this policy sector, central government is responsible for determining the overarching goals of planning policy (e.g. provision of enough housing to meet demand and protection of valued natural environments) and formulating the means to achieve those goals. During the period under study here (1990-2000) the main means used by government in achieving these goals were housing projections and a plan-led policy approach. In the projections, the central state calculates likely housing requirements in England for a period of twenty years. It produces a national figure for the required new houses and this provides the basis for planning policy. In short, the planning system is charged with ensuring that sufficient land is forthcoming to meet the housing requirement. In order to execute this policy, the national figure is then 'parcelled out' to the regions so that each region takes a share of the national total. Similarly, the regional total is 'parcelled out' to the counties and then ultimately to the districts. In this way the figures cascade down the system from 'top' to 'bottom'. Thus, planning is oriented to ensuring the delivery of new housing.

There is a strong interrelationship between the cascading figures and the tiers of government in planning for housing. This has led many commentators to propose that the planning for housing system is centrally directed, with the inference being that all the other tiers simply fall into line (e.g. Murdoch *et al.*, 1999; Vigar *et al.*, 2000). However, in the plan-led system, these other tiers have responsibilities and pressures that mean 'falling into line' can be problematic. In particular, the political and social pressures bearing upon regional and local plans (notably from the environmental lobby and new rural residents) may mean that there is resistance to the implementation of the figures and this resistance has somehow to be managed. The management of environmental resistance is a major theme of this book.

It is at the local level that the various political and social pressures that swirl around the provision of new housing become most evident. Using case study material gathered during two Economic and Social Research Council-funded research projects conducted in Buckinghamshire in the south east of England, we show how the housing projections cascade all the way down to the local level and how they emerge from complex processes of negotiation around local plans. The case study material stems from interviews with all the main actors in structure and local plan review processes. It also utilizes material drawn from an ethnographic study of a single village (Haddenham in Aylesbury Vale) which one of the authors (Abram) conducted in 1997. This work is presented in Chapters 5 and 6.

In Chapter 5, we study the formulation of a structure (that is, county level) plan and show how the housing figures were incorporated into plan policies. We also examine discourses of development and environment within the plan-making process and illustrate how the housing projections acted to constrain and direct the arguments. In Chapter 6, we consider how the figures moved on down to the district level and the arguments that broke out around them. Although a variety of local actors sought to prevent any significant amount of new housing being enshrined in the district plan, they soon discovered that there was very little scope for negotiation around the overall numbers. In the case study, the debates tended to focus upon the planned location of new housing, notably its distribution between urban and rural areas. We analyse these debates from the vantage point of a rural village (Haddenham), one which was expected to take a substantial amount of new housing development. We show how conflicts emerged within the village over the best way to resist this 'threat' and the way these conflicts shaped the village's response. We also highlight how the campaign against new housing became caught up in local politics and we consider the effect of local political manoeuvring upon the distribution of housing across the district.

In the main, then, the book focuses upon the relationship between planning policy and spatial context. It aims to show how policy pushes certain goals (e.g. provision of new housing to meet the requirements of future households) and how these come into conflict with the goals of those who are invited to consider the plans and the policies (e.g. environmentalists and rural residents) at the regional and local levels. This conflict is summarized as a struggle between the agents of development and the agents of environmental protection.

In the final chapter, Chapter 7, we consider whether the conflict between the two sets of discourses is leading to some reshaping of the policy hierarchy. A Labour Government came into power in 1997 with little obvious interest in planning but soon found itself embroiled in the planning for housing dispute (Allmendinger and Tewdwr-Jones, 2000). As a consequence, it has set about re-orienting policy in order to achieve a better balance between development and environment. In the process it has begun to accentuate the significance of the regional planning tier. Thus, some 're-jigging' of the hierarchical relations in planning seems to be underway. In Chapter 7 we consider whether these changes will ameliorate the conflicts that have been outlined in earlier chapters. We show that while recent policy initiatives may get central government off the political 'hook' of being seen as responsible for the large numbers of new houses appearing across the countryside, these initiatives may also have unforeseen consequences, most notably a shortage of houses. The spectacle of a Labour Government putting protection of the countryside before the building of new houses is, in some respects, quite remarkable; this book might be read as an account of how this situation came into being.

Some theoretical guidelines

In this section we outline a number of theoretical ideas that will inform the analysis and which we believe will help to show how a coherent policy line in planning for housing meshes with the various tiers of government according to the precepts of certain 'rationalities'. In so doing, we briefly consider two theoretical bodies of work associated with the terms *governance* and *governmentality*. We employ these concepts to analyse the interaction between a hierarchical system of regulation and the agencies of government operating within that system.

We begin with the term 'governance'. This concept has emerged in political science in order to account for a move away from the top-down, bureaucratic styles of policy making associated with 'government'. Recent studies of the policy process have recognized that, in the formulation and implementation of policy, the state's various agencies may be loosely co-ordinated (or may even be working against each other), so that policy emerges from a variety of governmental sites. Analysts of the policy process have thus begun to adopt a multi-agency perspective in order to uncover how the various policy actors both co-ordinate their actions and compete with one another. This has led to an interest in both 'policy networks' – that is, the coalitions between actors (Rhodes, 1997) – and 'multi-level governance' – that is, the way policy ties together the different tiers of the state (Marks, 1996). In short, the 'governance' perspective sees political action emerging from a host of governmental and non-governmental agencies (Goodwin, 1998; Stoker, 1998a).

According to Goodwin (1998), 'governance' now refers to the complex set of institutions and actors that are drawn from within, but also beyond, government in the process of policy formulation and implementation. The term thus suggests a blurring of boundaries and responsibilities between state and non-state actors and a recognition that the capacity to get things done does not rest solely on the power of governmental authority (see also Stoker, 2000). Thus, old-style government - that is, top-down, hierarchical decision making in the context of the policy process - is thought to be much less effective in carrying through state programmes and policies and it gives way to a form of policy making that works through networks and partnerships.

The governance literature stems from a number of (not always commensurate) theoretical positions (see Vigar *et al.*, 2000 for an alternative review to that provided below). Smith (2000) mentions two as being of particular interest: policy network analysis and the advocacy coalition framework. As Smith shows, both these theoretical perspectives emphasize the importance of inter-organisational relationships within policy sectors. Because modern policy problems are complex, and because few agencies have the wherewithal to intervene decisively in any particular policy arena, coalitions are needed for any policy action to be effectively executed. In line with the 'governance' perspective, policy network analysis assumes that 'policymaking is sectoralized and takes place within networks of public and private policy actors' (Smith, 2000 p.96). This approach places these networks on a continuum, one that extends from tightly-knit 'policy communities' - which contain 'a limited number of well-resourced members enjoying a common appreciative system, and exhibiting regular interaction and exchange between members' (2000 p.97) - to loosely aligned 'issue networks' - where 'membership encompasses a wide range of interests even though members may have limited resources' (*Ibid.*). The differing network types impact upon policy in differing ways and ensure that quite different policy formulation and implementation processes exist within any given political formation (John, 1998).

The advocacy coalition approach also examines the structure of governance systems but points to shared beliefs and policy-oriented learning processes as the salient features of political coalitions. Smith (2000 p.98) summarizes the position in the following way:

> The essential premise of the advocacy coalition framework is that policy making occurs in a policy subsystem inhabited by several multi-actor advocacy coalitions which compete to influence policy in line with the policy beliefs which bind each coalition together... The process of competition between advocacy coalitions generates policy-oriented learning. The [advocacy coalition framework] conceives policy change as a relatively open and competitive process between belief systems.

For policy network analysis, policy change occurs as a result of both interaction between networks and changes in external (or environmental) conditions (Marsh and Smith, 2000).

These two frameworks emphasize that modern political systems are fragmented, with coalitions and networks - which are composed of state and non-state actors and which are bound together through either shared beliefs or resource-dependencies (Rhodes, 1997) - competing to influence processes and outcomes. The coalitions and networks provide some (relative) stability in the political system and act to 'embed' the state in a rich array of 'external' relations. Thus, theories of 'governance' hold that the state has shifted from being both the formulator and deliverer of policy: it is now an 'orchestrator' (or 'conductor') of networks. While state agencies may arbitrate over policy, they can only act in relations with others.

In assessing the significance of the 'governance' approach for planning theory, Vigar *et al.* (2000) propose that it has led to the development of an 'institutionalist' perspective. According to these authors (2000 p.50), 'institutionalist analysis takes for granted that the social worlds of people in formal agencies of government are intertwined with wider social forces, embedding governance processes in wider relations of economic activity and civil society'.

They argue, therefore, that the planning system provides a set of arenas in which clusters of stakeholders, 'who share common frames of reference and substantive issues of concern' (2000 p.245), can come together to discuss the meaning and shape of policy. These stakeholders hold the capacity to develop linkages with other actors in these arenas (in the form perhaps of 'policy networks' or 'advocacy coalitions') so that planning strategies can be developed which reflect their aspirations.

Vigar *et al.*, explicitly link this institutionalist perspective to a more territorially-sensitive form of planning: 'The objective [is] to replace vertical and sectoral relationships with territorial ones and to build up a capacity to build strategic policy frameworks to guide and co-ordinate the actions of a multiplicity of stakeholders in territorial development' (2000 p.4). Thus, rather than top-down determination of planning policy, the new governance system should enable 'disparate actors in dispersed governance contexts [to] come together to build consensus around difficult local and developmental issues' (2000 p.46). Vigar *et al.* discern potential 'for the formation of new policy communities with different foci, including a territorial development perspective'.

While they recognize that a governance framework would, in theory, allow a new spatial planning approach to come into being, Vigar *et al.*, believe the current structure of the UK planning system works against such a shift. In concluding their study of planning in three English regions, they (2000 p.246) claim their findings show 'the continuing power of vertical relations, combined with a narrowing of the remit of the planning system, thus reducing the pressure to develop rich horizontal linkages'. The place-based system that they advocate is thus inhibited by a continuing set of top-down vertical linkages. The challenge from a governance perspective is therefore 'to shift the inherited institutional structure from the trajectory into which it has been channelled... into a richer, more place-focused, more future-oriented and more localized form' (2000 p.289).

In important respects, then, it appears as though continuity in policy as it cascades down the governmental tiers is more important than the differences imposed by loosely connected agencies of governance. For this reason we believe it may be worth tempering the focus on 'governance' through a consideration of 'governmentality', a concept originally developed by Michel Foucault (1991; see also Barry *et al.*, 1996; Gordon, 1991; McNay, 1994). As Dean (1999 p.18) puts it, Foucault believed the 'analysis of government is concerned with thought as it becomes linked to, and is embedded in, technical means for the shaping and reshaping of conduct in practices and institutions'. Foucault used the term 'governmentality' to refer to the collective ways of thinking that underpin particular governmental strategies and the means by which such strategies are operationalized. Like the theorists of 'governance', Foucault believed that the state can only govern in and through networks and coalitions. However, he prioritized the role of discourse and the 'mentalities of rule' that lie within state-inspired discourses in accounting for network forms.

In developing Foucault's ideas, Miller (1990) has argued that the governmentality approach allows government to be analysed as the composite of differing practices and discourses. He identifies, firstly, *political rationalities* which he describes as

> the field of statements, claims and prescriptions that set out the objects and objectives of government. Objects such as the "economy" or "society" are entities that have been constructed and made intelligible according to a particular way of thinking them as an economy or a society (1990 p.137).

This is accomplished through the production of discursive matrices that define a common vocabulary and that specify the appropriate bases for the organisation and mobilisation of social and political actors. Furthermore, the adoption of shared vocabularies enables associations to be formed between a variety of actions and agents dispersed in space and time:

> ...departments of State, pressure groups, academics, managers, teachers, employees, parents - whilst each remains, to a greater or lesser extent, constitutionally distinct and formally independent... can be enrolled in a governmental network to the extent that it can translate the objectives and values of others into its own terms, to the extent that the arguments of another become consonant with and provide norms for its own ambitions (Miller and Rose, 1990 p.6).

According to Rose (1991 p.28), political rationalities allow conclusions to be reached about 'what should be done, by whom and how'. In this respect, the governmentality approach shares something in common with the policy network and advocacy coalition frameworks for it too examines how political networks coalesce around governmental discourses. What differentiates it is the emphasis it places on a second aspect of political network building - the *mechanisms* or *technologies* which permit discourses to be stabilized in particular sets of political relations (Dean, 1999; Rose, 1999).

Any governmentality - to be effective - requires that the objects and objectives of government are rendered amenable to intervention. Thus techniques and technologies are required that can 'materialize and visualize (the) processes and activities to be regulated' (Miller and Rose, 1990 p.317). More generally,

> all government depends on a particular mode of "representation": the elaboration of a language for the depicting of the domain in question that claims both to grasp the nature of reality represented and literally to represent it in a form amenable to political deliberation, argument and scheming (1990 p.6).

These comments draw attention to those components of policy that might be termed 'knowledge' - the techniques and vocabularies that make aspects of policy calculable and amenable to deliberate and planned initiatives. In sum, governmentality describes the means by which government both 'represents' and 'intervenes' in the world (Hacking, 1981).

As Rose (1999 p.48) puts it, specific governmentalities allow alignments to be forged 'between the objectives of authorities wishing to govern and the personal projects of those organisations, groups and individuals who are the subjects of government'. Linkages are assembled so that both governmental agencies and free citizens are aligned and their behaviours interlocked. Government thus operates through non-political modes of authority. It is conducted - as Rose (1999) says - through 'lines of force' which span both political and non-political domains.

We are drawn to this approach because it seems to us that key modes of governmentality are instrumental in linking together the various tiers of the planning hierarchy. Thus, the governmentality approach might usefully complement the focus on 'governance'. Where one stresses the establishment of 'lines of force' across domains, the other emphasizes the room for discretion in differing political arenas. Policy might therefore be characterized as subject to a constant struggle between, on the one hand, the construction of tightly regulated networks that permit central agencies to determine the actions of all network members and, on the other, loosely connected agencies which reshape policy in line with their own locally constructed preferences. And in planning, this struggle emerges not just around the powers to be attributed to the various governmental tiers but also around the amount of spatial sensitivity to be permitted in the system. As Vigar *et al.*, (2000) make clear, 'governance' in planning means an enhanced role for territorially-based networks and coalitions in the determination of policy; old-style 'government' seems to imply the dominance of a centrally imposed and uniform policy.

Space versus time in the planning sector

The degree to which the planning system is sensitive to the needs and demands of particular spatial areas is, to a considerable extent, shaped by the interaction between formal systems of governance and the practices of those who run such systems (Marsh and Smith, 2000; Vigar *et al.*, 2000). However, this interaction is, in turn, shaped by the amalgam of political rationalities and technical expertise that runs through planning. For instance, planning uses a whole raft of techniques that determine planning practice. It is often assumed that, to some extent at least, these techniques are free from political influence. In one sense, then, planning is a *technical* activity (Mazza, 1995). Yet planning is also a *political* activity and it must gain political legitimacy for the decisions taken by planning agencies (Tewdwr-Jones, 1995). The distinction between the 'technical' and the 'political' in planning is an uneasy one for, as we shall see in the following chapters, political negotiation often leads to the adoption of new techniques that in some way incorporate political compromises while techniques can foreclose political choices. The adoption of particular techniques can thus become the subject of political dispute so that the boundary between the 'technical' and the 'political' regularly moves.

The political/technical divide, despite its shifting nature, remains central to any understanding of planning practice, not least because it bears upon the amount of genuinely 'spatial' planning permitted in the system. The use of particular technologies can foreclose the scope for political network building in territorial arenas. We will illustrate this issue in the following chapters by pointing to a governmental technology that is central in planning for housing - the use of numbers.

According to Rose (1991), numbers are ubiquitous in modern government. They are frequently used in both formulating governmental programmes and in putting these programmes into action. He argues that statistics and other numerical techniques have become integral to governmental practice because they promise a 'privileged vantage point' from which to view the domain to be governed. As he says: 'Through the development of such complex relays of inscription and accumulation [as numbers], new conduits of power are brought into being between those who wish to exercise power and those over whom they wish to exercise it' (1991 p.676).

Rose (1991 p.674) stresses that, in part, statistics are attractive tools for modern governments because they provide stability and recurrence in the knowledge resources available to the state (see also Kallinikos, 1996). Stability and recurrence permit 'action at a distance' (Latour, 1987). Governmental networks can act particularly effectively when they pull information about the world towards the state's 'centres of calculation'; the networks can refine modes of intervention in the light of the information thereby gathered in. Latour (1987 p.223) argues that governmental technologies function in this fashion because they have certain characteristics: firstly, they are mobile so that they carry information back to a centre of calculation; secondly, they have the ability to remain stable so that the information is moved back and forth without 'distortion, disruption or decay'; and, thirdly, they are capable of aggregation so that information is condensed (Latour, 1987 p. 223).

These technological forms are stable and robust enough to move through multiple situations without losing their shapes and functions and they thereby ensure that localized actions are both known and 'acted upon'. This point is relevant to our main case study: the planning for housing policy sector is marked out by a 'cascade' of numbers which links together actors and agencies at various tiers of government (Abram *et al.*, 1998; Murdoch *et al.*, 1999; Murdoch, 2000; Vigar *et al.*, 2000). The figures, in a Foucauldian sense, act in ways that 'discipline' the behaviour of actors in a variety of local contexts (thereby restricting the scope for 'spatial governance'). However, it is clear that while the figures have disciplinary effects, they also open up scope for disputation by making future development trajectories visible. As they 'combine', 'aggregate' and 'shuffle' complex layers of information, so they simplify the various economic and social processes surrounding development and allow a broad array of actors to discern their significance. Moreover, the planning system itself provides forums for challenging (or 'testing') the figures, so that interested actors are encouraged to counter the various development policies (we examine these challenges in chapters 5 and 6). And these challenges take a spatial form: that is, actors entering these local forums seek to bring the figures down to 'earth'; they wish to drag them out of the abstract realm in which they are initially constructed and embed them in real, spatial contexts. It is thus important that the relationship between governmentality and space is investigated.

Another way that this distinction between technical 'abstraction' and 'spatialization' might be conceptualized is as a distinction between 'space' and 'time' (see Murdoch, 2000). As Latour (1987) emphasizes, categories such as numbers are adopted within networks because they keep entities and elements stable as they are transported over spatial and temporal distances back to centres of calculation (e.g. state agencies). Interruptions may, however, either slow down or completely undermine the transportation of distant places or times back to the calculating centre (Latour, 1997). In this respect, the abstract can get 'bogged down' in the concrete (the local): it no longer 'hovers' above particular socio-spatial contexts, creating its own set of space-times, but is contaminated by complexity and contingency. In other words, the time encoded in the categories will fail to run smoothly over space; spaces and places will thereby be enhanced at the expense of categorized, abstracted, times. The deeper the immersion in local spaces, in their complexity and contingency, the slower the process of transporting abstractions, categorisations and so on, from one place to another.

The same thing occurs with the housing numbers: the numbers run along the governmental networks (and, in the process, help to tie those networks together) in order to ensure that sufficient houses are built to meet projected demand. Thus, the numbers - and the governmental networks that facilitate their functioning - are primarily concerned with development and time (the calculation of future households in present-day plans). Those actors seeking to resist the disciplinary effects of numbers argue that they must be embedded in local environments so that other issues of importance (e.g. nature and community) can be taken into account. In the planning for housing sphere, the distinction between development and environment thus turns into a distinction between time (abstraction) and space (local complexity). Throughout this book we indicate how these distinctions are assessed and maintained in the arenas of planning.

As we shall see, at the present time the way planning for housing policy deals with these issues appears to be changing. There now seems to be some sympathy in government for the need to take spatial circumstances much more fully into consideration at regional and local levels. However, such sympathies raise afresh the role of the numbers: are the projections of housing demand to be used to determine decisions or are they simply one of many factors to be taken into consideration when deciding levels of housing development in a given area over a given time period? The case study material presented in this book indicates that the answer provided to this question will be crucial in determining not only the numbers of houses that will be built but also the state of England's rural environment.

Conclusion

Recent trends and debates in the planning policy sector highlight an uneasy tension between coherent, ubiquitous forms of regulation that draw all tiers of government into a single regime of policy, and looser configurations in which differing governmental tiers have scope to develop policies in ways that best suit their particular (economic, social, political and environmental) circumstances. This tension is superimposed on another: policy as an abstract, widely dispersed and generalized set of prescriptions and policy as the outcome of many spatially embedded, territorially sensitive approaches. These two tensions run through contemporary planning policy.

The key issue here is how far planning policy is to be embedded in spatial formations at different territorial scales. In the main, planning is an abstract and technical activity. Such characteristics can serve to detach the practice of planning (despite it primary concern for spatial management) from any deep spatial belonging (e.g. policy as the reflection of local circumstances). Yet, the environmental challenge is leading to the assertion of a new spatial sensitivity, one that seeks to ensure that, within give territories, plans take into account rich mixtures of the natural, the social and the economic (see Graham and Healey, 1999). Thus, rather than imposing development in ways that correspond to the simplified spaces of the planner's imagination, the challenge for planning is to ensure that a whole array of spatial entities are considered when formulating development policies and plans. And these entities should be incorporated into planning's discursive repertoire, not just in terms of their effect on particular developments, but as things with their own forms of 'intrinsic' value. In other words, planners should think of environments, natures, social needs and economic demands etc. in a 'symmetrical' fashion (Latour, 1993), so that clear and reasoned justifications for privileging one over the others are given in all circumstances. These 'clear and reasoned justifications' will begin from the starting point that spatial complexity is to be encouraged rather than diminished and that planning's main role is to promote rich 'mixtures' of nature/society. Development will therefore have to be assessed against this yardstick.

In what follows, we argue that the new concern for 'space' or 'environment' in planning follows from some long-standing trends within the planning sector, trends which appear to be congealing into a new rationality - 'spatial planning' or 'planning for sustainable development'. By 'rationality' here we mean a discursive formation in which arguments cohere in ways that make them ultimately almost unquestionable. In other words, they become 'black boxes' or 'positive modalities' (Murdoch *et al.*, 1999), in which all the tensions, contradictions, precarious alliances, alternative forms of reasoning that may have gone into their making 'disappear'. The uncertainties disappear and the modalities reach the status of 'facts'. Within these 'facts', a whole host of resources and entities are stitched together in ways that make them hard to challenge. As Latour (1987) puts it, the legitimising arguments and resources are piled up like the banks of the river thereby ensuring that the flow of argumentation is always towards the desired conclusion – the 'fact'.

Rationalities are 'simplifications' of the contexts in which they are embedded. As simplifications they can be detached from particular contexts and can then act in a diverse range of circumstances (although they can only do this if the networks that transport them around remain stable; as we shall see the planning network has remained so stable that differing rationalities have come to compete with one another). Once these simplifications become disembedded then, in our terms, they reach the status of rationalities and act back upon the initial conditions. Thus, rationalities are recursively related to the contexts in which they emerge. Once a set of facts, debates, alliances, political assumptions have stabilized in a coherent fashion then they can go on to frame other debates, alliances, assumptions and modes of organisation. By achieving the status of taken-for-granted policy goals, rationalities can become powerful actors or 'modes of ordering' (Law, 1994) in a range of political circumstances.

These rationalities are, therefore, both reflective and constitutive of network relations. The rationality and the network co-construct one another, so that a new rationality would also reflect/constitute new network relations. Rather than representing a form of context-independent reason, Ouroussoff argues that 'the rationalist framework constitutes local native theory' (2001 p.38). With reference to Sahlins, she adds that, 'rationality is how we explain ourselves to ourselves: it is our rationalization' (*ibid.*). There is a parallel here with the '*real rationality*' (c.f. realpolitik) that Flybjerg distinguishes from formal rationality, using a model by which 'power defines rationality and power defines reality' (1998 p.36). He suggests that while formal rationality is one of the few forms of power accessible to those without influence, it holds no guarantee of influence over outcomes. What influences decisions is what he terms real rationality, a form of post-hoc rationalization in which the results of negotiations, influence and pressure are concealed behind descriptions of outcomes as rational or technically-logical solutions. These rationalizations hold together networks of powerful actors, and simultaneously define the power that these actors have, through the stability of the rationality. They are both outcomes and contexts in themselves.

This notion of rationality takes the discursive components of the advocacy coalition approach and the networking aspects of policy network theory but extends them using the governmentality repertoire. We can therefore see rationalities as made up of multiple discursive components (e.g. the technical and the political). These discursive 'assemblages' are situated both within and beyond state networks or coalitions. They travel via the governmental 'lines of force' that configure particular policy areas; these 'lines' - as Rose (1999) argues - align both state and non-state actors. We shall argue that the new rationality of 'spatial' or 'sustainable development' has now become 'disembedded' and is being promoted in diverse quarters - by professional planners and academics eager to find a new role for planning expertise, by new rural residents keen to protect their neighbourhoods against further development, by environmental groups concerned at the impact of economic growth on natural environments, and by politicians seeking to ameliorate some of the contradictory pressures that bear upon them. The concerns of all these participants appear to be defining a new rationality within planning and planning policy. 'Spatial' or 'sustainable' development reflects and refines the various aspirations of these groups.

In the context of our case study, the gradual coherence of this new rationality leads to the emergence of a 'trade-off' between, on the one hand, the spatialisation or contextualisation of planning for housing policy and, on the other, the maintenance of its ability to meet economic and social demands. We argue that the balance between planning's rationalities is precarious at the present time. Yet, the way the 'trade off' is executed is of fundamental importance to the way people live, the way they are housed, and the state of the natural environment. In other words, how the contest between the rationality of development and the rationality of environment is resolved will determine whether housing can once again be seen as a 'public good' or whether it must continue to be cast as a form of 'pollution'.

Chapter 2

The Changing Rationalities of Planning Policy

Introduction

In this book we examine the changing political and institutional context surrounding planning policy in the UK, and also the changing content of the policies themselves. In this, the first substantive chapter, we provide an overview of planning policy and introduce two main topics in order to guide the review. Firstly, we say something about the changing shape of planning, especially in the context of its institutional structure. We briefly review some the key trends and issues that have emerged over the last twenty years or so in order to set later chapters in a longer historical context. Secondly, and leading on from this brief historical reflection, we say something about the changing content of planning policies and ultimately plans themselves. We relate the changes in policy to changes in the context of planning. The contextual changes are of two types: political and social. We thus outline how differing political interpretations of planning emerged and show how these were linked to social changes (notably growing awareness of environmental issues and an increase in the rural population).

Our main focus here is the balance between developmental and environmental considerations and the purpose of this chapter is to show how the debate between the two discourses was conditioned by a range of processes - political, economic, social, environmental. These various processes had a decisive impact on the status of the two rationalities of development and environment. In subsequent chapters we will examine how the rationalities run down the tiers of government, while in chapters 5 and 6 we show how they shape planning debates in particular local areas. The main purpose of the present chapter, however, is to argue that, while planning policy provides the framework within which disputes between development and environment are played out, planning policy itself is conditioned by these disputes. There is, therefore, a recursive relationship between policy and context.

The first part of the chapter surveys planning policy during the 1980s and describes the emphasis that was placed on the market and thus upon development. It then goes on to chart a shift back to environment-led planning during the 1990s under the governments of John Major and Tony Blair. As we shall see, changes made during this period gave rise to a new policy goal derived from the new discourse of sustainability. The emergence of this goal can be linked to two inter-linked trends: increased participation in a plan-led system and counterurbanization. Each is described in turn. This brief survey of these different phases of planning provides a context for subsequent chapters.

The general argument presented here proposes that during the last twenty years or so planning has been forced to become more attuned to environmental and spatial complexity (see also Healey and Shaw, 1994). Various trends have unfolded in ways that have pushed environment and territory onto the policy agenda. Thus, despite occasional shifts towards market- or development-led planning, the general tenor of planning policy is greater sensitivity to spatial and environmental issues. However, as we shall see in more detail in Chapter 3, this has not yet resulted in a fundamental redistribution of responsibilities between the governmental tiers involved in planning policy. Thus, while a new rationality of planning ('sustainable development') is currently emerging, it must take its place in a relatively unchanged planning hierarchy. As subsequent chapters show, tensions are currently arising as result of planning's new environmental or spatial sensitivity and the relatively unchanging structure of policy delivery.

Planning in the 1980s

It is fair to say that, in many respects, planning has been through a turbulent time in the last couple of decades. Many commentators trace the beginning of this turbulence to the election of Mrs Thatcher in 1979. In the second edition of his book *Urban Planning under Thatcherism*, Thornley (1993) points out that, as a component of the welfare state, a component that permitted government to intervene in the operation of land markets in pursuit of the 'public good', planning was in a vulnerable position following Mrs Thatcher's election victory. Essentially the Thatcher governments were of the view that competitive markets guarantee the best outcomes and therefore these markets should, wherever possible, be substituted for state activity. This underlying ideological predisposition bred a distrust and dislike of state activity, particular in those areas of political life that central government did not directly control, most notably local government. Thus, planning - which was viewed as both a local government activity and a potential hindrance to market operations - was not looked upon kindly by the incoming Conservative government. Atkinson and Moon (1994 p.183) quote Michael Heseltine - who was the Environment Minister at the beginning of Mrs Thatcher's first government - as saying in a speech to the Royal Town Planning Institute (RTPI) in 1979:

> This country cannot afford the manpower involved in a [planning] system which in some parts can be negative and unresponsive. But above all we cannot afford the economic process of delayed investment, whether commercial, domestic or industrial.

Planning, it was argued, inhibits entrepreneurship and risk taking, it stifles new economic activities, and drapes industry in regulation and 'red tape'. In the planning field, as in many other areas of social, economic and political life, the Thatcher government believed fundamental change was needed so that the activities of the state could be reined in and the operation of the market could be expanded. The Adam Smith Institute, a right wing think tank popular with Conservative governments during the period, argued in 1983 that the planning system should be partially dismantled (although it believed some urban and rural conservation and public health legislation should be retained) because other control mechanisms - such as economic forces, private institutional controls (e.g. covenants) and central government regulation - would work much more effectively. Planning could still play a role in the regulation of development, but it should act as an interpreter of market signals rather than a prescriptive regulator. It should ensure the smooth functioning of markets (such as through the provision of infrastructure).

Two main modifications to the planning system were mooted at this time: on the one hand, the market should be given more free play while, on the other, central state regulation should replace local government regulation. Thornley (1993) argues that, effectively, the Thatcher governments set about trying to either circumvent completely the town and country planning machinery or to replace existing legislation with new measures of a more streamlined kind. In short, the Conservatives sought to restructure the planning system in line with private sector demands; they therefore legitimized the developmental discourse (Allmendinger and Tewdwr-Jones, 1997).

The landmark legislative achievement of the first Thatcher government was the Local Government, Planning and Land Act of 1980 (Atkinson and Moon, 1994). The Act both outlined early Thatcherite changes to the system and signalled the expected directions of policy development. Atkinson and Moon (1994) note three main themes running through the Act. First, the position of county councils and the status of structure plans should be weakened so that development control powers could be consolidated at the district level (except for minerals and waste disposal, which would remain with the counties). The effect of this proposal would be to diminish the policy formulation and implementation powers of county councils. Moreover, district councils would be given the freedom to formulate local plans without the prior approval accorded by structure plans. The Act was thus interpreted as a shift in the balance of power between counties and districts in favour of the latter (Thornley, 1993 p.126). Secondly, the Act sought to make plans more efficient and more attuned to market requirements by speeding up the plan making process. Speed and simplification were required, it was argued, to keep down cost and to exclude unnecessary areas of regulation. Participation was also to be pruned to ensure greater speed of preparation. Thirdly, the Act began to elaborate a set of procedures for by-passing the statutory system altogether. Under the legislation, the Secretary of State for the Environment was given the power to designate certain inner city areas as 'urban development zones', with their own Urban Development Corporations (UDCs). The UDCs were given full development control powers in these areas (so that the local authorities effectively lost jurisdiction over planning). The new corporations subsumed 'all the powers formerly exercized by the various authorities for the area at borough and district and strategic level' (Grant, 1982, quoted in Thornley, 1993 p.167).

We see here an attempt to make the planning system more responsive to the private-sector (by speeding up plan-making). There was also an effort to weaken certain aspects of the local state either by downgrading the powers of local government (as in the case of the counties) or by implementing local policies outside the state itself (for instance, through the UDCs). This general approach was continued throughout the early and mid-1980s, notably in the Local Government Act of 1985 which effectively abolished the metropolitan county councils of the major cities and transferred their statutory powers to metropolitan districts and boroughs. The planning system was also transferred to the new authorities, with new Unitary Development Plans replacing the previous system. Outside the metropolitan areas, however, the two tier (structure and local plan) system remained in the force.

In 1985 a white paper was produced with the poignant title *Lifting the Burden*. The aim of this document was to promote a curtailment of those systems of regulation which were believed to be inhibiting the growth of private-sector business and slowing the recovery of the economy. The 'burden', it was suggested, arose as a consequence of the way planning interferes in market operations. Again, it was stated that the planning system should be simplified. Development plans should be seen as useful planning tools but only because they 'can assist developers and the business community by providing them with some indicators to guide them in taking decisions' (quoted in Thornley, 1993 p.135). Moreover, the White Paper emphasized that 'development plans are one, but only one, of the material considerations that must be taken into account in dealing with planning applications' (*ibid.*). The document went on to say that

> it is also important that development plans should concentrate on the essential elements and the key planning issues, be well related to current trends in the economy and the factors that influence market demand, and be capable of rapid revision to meet changing circumstances (quoted in Thornley, 1993 p.136).

Again, there is an attempt to downgrade the status of development plans in the face of the principal material consideration, that of encouraging economic growth (similar sentiments were also expressed in the Green Paper *The Future of Development Plans* published in 1986).

Of particular concern to the Conservatives was the complexity of the plan making process, notably the split between structure and district plans. Thus, by the late 1980s rumours began to circulate that structure plans were to be abolished. These sentiments came to the fore in the 1989 White Paper *The Future of Development Plans* where again it was emphasized that planning should aid economic development, while protecting and conserving the best of the natural and urban fabric. As Thornley (1993 p.141) says, 'the emphasis is very much on responding to the dynamic market with the proviso that some areas may require protection'. Once again, the need was identified for swift responses and flexibility in the system: 'The paper identified three basic problems with the existing structure: the scope of the policies, the relationship between structure and local plans and the complexity of the procedures' (*ibid.*). Structure plans in particular were seen as far too broad and 'include policies that have nothing to do with land use planning or improving the physical environment' (*ibid.*). It was thus asserted that local plans should provide the basic plan framework within loose constraints set by central and county level guidance, although, once again it was argued that these should be produced more quickly, with less participation required. The White Paper therefore continued Conservative attempts to streamline the planning system so as to make it more responsive to the market economy (Brindley *et al.*, 1989). It also gave further evidence of the government's hostility to local government and demonstrated their continuing efforts to curtail local government activities, most notably in the continual weakening of the status of plans and planning.

In short, plan-making was not favoured by Conservative governments during the 1980s. In the view of most ministers, development plans inhibited market forces and plan making and should therefore be kept to a minimum. Reflecting on this aspect of Conservative thinking, Vigar *et al.* (2000 p.17) say:

> In the 1980s, national government, influenced by its neo-liberal ideology, was ambiguous about the role of development plans. Civil servants criticized structure plans for their cumbersome methodology and failure to focus on key strategic issues. The new ministers of the Tory administration objected to the interventionist stance the plans seemed to represent, challenged the potential of structure plans and local plans to develop policy directions of their own and, with little understanding of the problems of uncertainty in the development process, preferred to focus attention at the level of the project. The level of regional guidance was reduced to a minimum and, after a struggle in which the structure plan came near to abolition... it was proposed that development plans should focus primarily on detailing national policy as it affected localities.

As this quote makes clear, in seeking to curtail the power of development plans Conservative administrations redefined the relationship between central and local government in planning, with the centre securing the wherewithal to direct local policies.

In summarizing the effects of Conservative legislation in the 1980s Thornley (1993 p.209) says:

> underlying the initiatives was a desire to "free up" the planning system thereby giving greater scope for developers and house builders. This market

freedom is the essential ethic of the Urban Development Corporations, the Enterprise Zones and the Simplified Planning Zones. Many of the modifications to the planning system remove constraints on developers, for example, the relaxation of controls on industry and small business or the changes to the Use Classes Order. Part of the process of giving greater freedom to the market has involved the downgrading of alternative decision-making tools such as plans and policies. Such statements have been reduced in significance, as they have become only one "material consideration" alongside market pressures and demands.

In concluding his study Thornley (1993 p.217) argues that Thatcherite changes to planning can be summarized as a re-orientation of the purpose of planning towards greater acceptance of market forces, selective application of environmental criteria, and the removal of social concerns (such as the 'community interest') from planning policy.

The Thatcher governments effectively promoted a discourse of 'developmentalism' in planning and sought to strengthen the prescriptive powers of the central state, thereby diminishing the scope for territorial alliances or the introduction of spatialized complexity. This conclusion might lead us to assume that the planning system emerged into the 1990s in a profoundly altered state. Indeed, reflecting on these changes Tewdwr-Jones (1996 p.4) says that 'the effects of Thatcherism on the statutory planning system during the 1980s were widespread'. And yet, this is not the whole story for, as Thornley admits (1993 p.218), in many respects there were strong currents of continuity with earlier phases of planning policy during this period (see also Hull and Vigar, 1998). Moreover, the changes wrought by the Conservatives encountered a significant amount of opposition, which led to something of a backlash emerging in the late 1980s. As Healey and Shaw (1994 p.430) point out, 'the 1980s brought the conflicts between environmental conservation, management and development to the fore, as the introduction of neo-liberal political philosophy into central government thinking and market pressures came up against a maturing popular understanding of, and concern about, environmental issues...'. This shift in attitudes forced the Conservatives to retreat from the more wholesale restructuring of the planning system that they had envisaged in the early years of the decade. Moreover, it heralded the introduction of a new rationality of planning: 'planning for sustainable development'.

Post-Thatcherite planning

The backlash began to emerge in the middle years of the 1980s as local authorities started to object to the undermining of local democracy by central government (Allmendinger and Tewdwr-Jones, 1997). One aspect of this local authority lobbying against a diminution of their planning powers was a call for a return to a 'plan-led' system. However, what really mobilized a much larger constituency against the weakening of planning - and accelerated the introduction a plan-led approach - was the issue of house building in the south east of England, in particular the building of new settlements.

Economic growth in the south east region during the middle years of the decade had brought a growth in the demand for housing and other forms of development. Development demand was focused upon the outer suburban and rural areas of the south. As Ward (1994 p.250) puts it: 'The problem, especially severe for a Conservative government whose main support came from these very areas, was how to accommodate all this growth'. While the governments of the 1980s were primarily concerned with the promotion of enterprise - and, therefore, by extension, development - it soon became clear that the accommodation of development in the outer-metropolitan areas of the south was not susceptible to a free-market solution. As Ward put it, gradual, unplanned incremental growth 'spread the misery and political damage' (*ibid*.). Some concentration of development thus became necessary.

Filtered through the pro-market, pro-development prism of Thatcherite policy-making, concentration meant new towns or new settlements. Initial developments of this type - such as Lower Earley near Reading - seemed to indicate that they were the most appropriate solution to the continuing struggle between development and conservation in the outer south east. Encouraged by an apparent official sanctioning of this approach, a group of house builders came together within one company - Consortium Developments Ltd - with the express intention of creating new rural settlements and during the mid-1980s the company put forward a number of (now infamous) schemes, such as Tillingham Hall, Foxley Wood and Stone Basset. These were new towns designed to accommodate at least 5000 inhabitants and all were located in the south east of England. They were effectively a private sector solution to the problems of growth in the rural areas.

In order to facilitate the building of new settlements, the government was seeking ways to amend rural planning restrictions. However, tentative moves in this direction unleashed a storm of protest from rural environmental groups and residents of the rural south east, most of whom were natural Conservative Party supporters. Feelings came to a head when Nicholas Ridley, a notorious free-market ideologist and the then Secretary of State for the Environment, professed himself minded to allow one new settlement - Foxley Wood in Hampshire - to be built. Conservative Party voters gave vent to their feelings about this in the 1989 Euro-elections when the Green Party polled its highest ever share of the vote (15 per cent). More importantly, the Party did particularly well in the south east, for instance taking 19 per cent of the vote in the Thames Valley constituency.

This event prompted something of a change in direction for planning policy (see Marsden *et al*. 1993, Chapter 5 for a summary) as the government was finding it extremely hard to balance the requirements of development with the conservationist sensibilities of its electoral constituency. Thus, the pro-development Nicholas Ridley was replaced by Chris Patten, a much more pragmatic politician. The significance of this change in personnel was considerable. Allmendinger and Tewdwr-Jones (1997 p.103), in a review of planning policy during this period, say: 'The replacement of Nicholas Ridley as Environment Secretary with Chris Patten heralded a change in direction for government policy towards urban (and we might add, rural) planning'. In effect, it marked the limits of market-led development.

As Thornley points out in his postscript to the 1993 edition of *Urban Planning under Thatcherism*, the thrust of policy very quickly began to change. For instance, the proposal in *The Future of Development Plans* to replace structure plans with slim-line statements of county policy was dropped. Instead, the concept of 'local choice' was promoted, This principle was used to emphasize the value of the planning system in managing the environment. It also highlighted the importance of local communities in making their own decisions on the implementation of planning policy. According to Allmendinger and Tewdwr-Jones (1997 p.110).

> The ethos behind this concept was to directly transfer the development dilemma from central government to the local authorities. In future, instead of central government ministers taking responsibility for local decision-making and mediating between the two opposing sides, locally formulated and implemented development plans would have an enhanced status to meet local concerns through the democratic process.

'Local choice' was clearly expressed in the 1991 Planning and Compensation Act, which stipulated that all development-control decisions were now to be made in accordance with the development plan. The Act stated that 'in making any determination under the Planning Acts, regard is to be had to the development plan, the determination shall be made in accordance with the plan unless other material considerations indicate otherwise' (quoted in Thornley, 1993 p.229) In other words, the plan is not just *one* material consideration amongst others but became the *prime* consideration.

As well as this shift in the balance between the plan and other material considerations, there were changes to the nature of the plans themselves. Although structure plans were retained, they were slimmed down so that they concentrated upon a few key issues. Another change aimed at speeding up the system was that the new structure plans no longer required approval by the Secretary of State (county councils would undertake development plan reviews themselves). As far as local plans were concerned, the major change was that all districts would have to produce district-wide plans, to be reviewed every five years. For the first time local plans would include the whole district area (including rural areas) and would have an enhanced status vis-à-vis development-control decisions. This measure was generally interpreted as strengthening the role of local residents and conservation groups in determining the course of development (see Marsden *et al.*, 1993; Cullingworth and Nadin, 1997).

It is frequently argued that the 1991 Act indicates how planning policy came to take on some new and distinctive characteristics during the years of John Major's Conservative governments (e.g. Allmendinger and Tewdwr-Jones, 1997). The approach to development planning during the first half of the 1990s is characterized as a reversal of the market-led approach and is seen as a move towards a more 'plan-led' system in which the status of both local planning authorities and their plans was enhanced (Allmendinger and Tewdwr-Jones, 1997 p.109). In other words, local planning was strengthened. However, it is also argued that central direction of local planning was simultaneously enhanced at this time. As Allmendinger and Tewdwr-Jones (1997 p.110) put it:

> Since the introduction of the "plan-led" system the government has viewed its Planning Policy Guidance series of documents as an increasingly vital component of the urban planning framework, a strategic system of policy documentation that extends across national, regional, county and local levels in Britain....The strategic function of national planning advice has therefore been recognized as part of the overriding duty of central government ministers for state direction. But in addition to providing national strategic direction, PPGs are also useful in providing a convenient way of monitoring the planning system across various spatial scales and thereby ensure that a high of uniformity is achieved in planning practice.

The enhanced status of PPGs (which were introduced in 1988 to provide concise and readily accessible sources of guidance to replace the confusing array of circulars and other instruments previously used by government) implies that local planning authorities must follow the statements within these notes in carrying out both local development plan formulation and development control duties. If they wish to depart from government polices, as enshrined in the PPGs, then local authorities must demonstrate the locally justified grounds for this departure. In other words, local plans can only develop their own particular priorities in exceptional circumstances. Thus, the PPG-led system seems to restrict the assertion of more territorial specificity in the planning sector. As Vigar *et al.* (2000 p.274) put it, the PPG-led approach

> works through the specification of largely decontextualized policy principles. These detach sites and projects from their local situations. They situate them in an institutional environment, often at odds with the perspectives of stakeholders involved in the local conflicts.

Thus, while the plan-led system opened out arenas in which spatially-sensitive views could be put forward, PPGs ensured a specification of policy criteria 'in such a way that it was difficult for local considerations to gain influence' (Vigar *et al.*, 2000 p.275).

Nevertheless, despite these criticisms, the PPG/plan-led approach indicates a strengthening of planning during the Major years. Thus, Allmendinger and Tewdwr-Jones (1997 p.112) conclude that

> the 1990s have seen a return to a more balanced approach that takes account of the other two preoccupations of the planning system: the environment and community needs. The market is now being emphasized as (though still the main one) of a number of concerns.

This countervailing set of trends have led some commentators to argue that change is more discussed than real within the planning system. Barry Cullingworth (1997a p.130) has noted that

> a remarkable feature of the [1947 Town and County Planning Act] is that it has survived largely intact over the 50 years since it was passed....This is quite different from the position in most areas of public policy, where there has been a transformation, as with education and health, transport and what used to be called "public utilities". These have been changed in structure scope and purpose: they would be largely unrecognizable to their founders.

In attempting to explain this continuity, Cullingworth (1997b) focuses on the strength of protectionist tendencies planning. He believes the widespread support for protection and conservation is itself an obstacle to change (as was demonstrated in the row around new settlements during the latter part of the 1980s). He says:

> Green belts, the restraint of urban growth and the protection of the countryside receive extensive, and sometimes vociferous, public support; not so the promotion of new settlements, or even the establishment of park and ride schemes in the urban fringe. In the British planning system, change is something to be resisted, rather than facilitated or even accepted (1997b p.948).

Cullingworth believes that successive governments have been cowardly in the face of this resistance to change. Even the radical, reforming Conservative governments of the 1980s, when confronted with a backlash against the market-led approach, found it was 'politically much more comfortable to allow local authorities to deal with... sensitive issues through the development plan system' (1997b pp.947-948). In Cullingworth's view, the discourse of environmentalism has always rivalled developmentalism in planning circles

A prime example of this resistance to change emerged during the later years of the second Major government when it was forecast (in 1995) that 4.4 million new households would emerge in the years between 1991 and 2016. A political furore opened up around this projected figure as many rural and environmental groups realized that if approximately 50% of the required houses were built outside the main conurbations, then policies of restraint and concentration would be threatened. Thus, a concerted campaign against the figure was mounted and this forced the Major Government to initiate a national debate on the implications. John Gummer, the then Secretary of State for the Environment, argued that the figure was reflective of real trends but he attempted to gloss over the likely impact by suggesting that perhaps 75 per cent of the new houses could go into existing urban areas, thereby downplaying the consequences for valued rural landscapes. However, many informed commentators (notably the Town and Country Planning Association - TCPA) pointed out that, on the best available estimates, less than half the total was likely to be accommodated in the cities, and therefore most of the development pressure would inevitably come to bear upon the outer south east (as we mentioned earlier, around 2 million households were thought likely to form in that area by 2016). Housing became, therefore, a subject of much heated argument during the middle years of the decade (see Breheny, 1999, for a summary).

Tony Blair's Labour government inherited this debate. While the new government was more likely than its Conservative predecessors to be sympathetic (in an ideological sense) to planning, it might also be expected to stand up more robustly to the strong preservationist forces that support the protection of the countryside (traditionally Labour has relied much less than the Conservatives upon shire county votes). However in responding to concerns about the implications of the 4.4. million figure, John Prescott, the Environment Secretary, followed John Gummer by arguing that most of the new houses should go in the main conurbations (he set the target at 60%). In order to facilitate this, he established an Urban Task Force (chaired by the architect Richard Rogers) to provide practical examples of how urban areas can be made to accommodate more houses (the Task Force's recommendations can be found in Urban Task Force, 1999). In other policy recommendations Prescott argued that the days of 'predict and provide' (that is, predict the number of houses needed and provide the land to build them) were over. In so doing, he appeared to suggest that spatial and environmental considerations should be given greater weight (e.g. DETR, 1998b) in planning for housing.

It is arguable, then, that in important respects the policies of the first Labour administration stemmed directly from the incremental reforms initiated by Chris Patten in the early 1990s (such continuities have been a general feature of Labour's general approach - see Seldon, 2001; for a commentary on this continuity in planning see - Allmendinger and Tewdwr-Jones, 2000). While such continuity may encourage the interpretation (favoured by Cullingworth, 1997a and b, amongst others) that little has changed in planning during this period, it is our view, to be outlined in more detail in subsequent chapters, that *incrementally* a new rationality of planning is coming into view. This rationality is less concerned with market-led development than with 'sustainable development'. It thus opens out the possibility of more 'territorial specificity' in planning policy and a reconfiguration of the governmental hierarchy.

Planning for sustainable development

In making any assessment of the future thrust of planning policy, attention must be directed to the obvious role now played by environmentalism, especially as we argue here that this aspect of planning is leading to a new rationality or 'mode of ordering' emerging (Law, 1994). In important respects, a concern for the environment might be thought to reinforce the preservationist trends already strongly present in the system (Cullingworth, 1997b; Hall *et al.*, 1973). Indeed, many commentators have simply assumed that a concern with environmental issues implies 'business as usual' for planning, i.e. a continued emphasis on concentration and protection (see the compelling evidence assembled by Elson *et al.*, 1998). Others, however, have proposed that sustainable development marks a 'coming of age' of environmentalism in the planning sector and is leading to a new planning rationality (e.g. Blowers and Evans, 1997). In this section we wish to assess this trend and weigh these two sets of arguments against each other.

A concern for the promotion of sustainable development has grown over the period being discussed here. The term began to emerge in international policy statements in the early 1980s and was most famously summarized in the Brundtland Report of 1987 (World Commission on Environment and Development, 1987). This report yielded probably the most common definition of sustainable development in use today: 'development that meets the needs of the present without compromising the ability of future generations to meet their own needs'. The term has subsequently been incorporated into policy discourses at many different tiers of government.

Initially, the British Government was slow to take an interest in this issue. Mrs Thatcher showed herself to be fairly hostile to environmental concerns (although she did exhibit, as Thornley, 1993 p.231, notes, an abiding concern with litter!). However, in the late 1980s - at about the time a backlash against Conservative planning policies was emerging - Mrs Thatcher began to change her views. In 1988 she delivered speeches which displayed a growing concern for global environmental problems (this was also the time when global climate change became widely publicized). As a result of this interest, and following the furore surrounding new settlements in the south east, Chris Patten produced *This Common Inheritance*, the first comprehensive policy document on the environment published by a British government. The document claimed to commit the government to pursuing the principles of sustainable development as set out in the Brundtland Report (these might be summarized as: conserving natural resources; enabling development and economic growth to take place in ways that preserve or enhance the environment; and maintaining environmental quality for future generations - see Quinn, 1996). Basically *This Common Inheritance* was a review of government policy in relation to sustainability; however it contained little in the way of concrete policies as, in the main, the Conservatives believed environmental solutions could be best delivered by market mechanisms rather than state policy.

Under John Major, and under commitments entered into at the 1992 Rio Earth Summit, the government began to focus a little more on how policies might bring patterns of more sustainable living and working into being. *This Common Inheritance* was thus followed in 1994 by *Sustainable Development: the UK Strategy*. The planning system was identified here as a key instrument for delivering sustainable land use and development. *Sustainable Development: the UK Strategy* argued that all local authorities - in the plan-led system - should prepare their plans taking environmental considerations fully into account. The government committed itself to ensuring that the principles of sustainable development permeated through the various governmental layers constituting the planning system. It also claimed it would encourage a host of sustainability objectives, including:

- Attractive and convenient urban areas, in which people will want to live and work.
- New development in locations which minimize energy consumption.
- The regeneration of urban land and buildings.
- Development to sustain the countryside.

These kinds of sentiments were already becoming evident in planning policy guidance notes: for instance, PPG 12 of 1992 contained a whole section devoted to environmental aspects, covering such things as global warming and the consumption of non-renewable resources. PPG 1 on *General Policy and Principles*, published in 1997, continued the theme. It argued that a key role for the planning system is 'to enable the provision of homes and buildings investment and jobs in a way which is consistent with the principles of sustainable development' (DETR, 1997 p.2). It stipulated that a sustainable planning framework should include:

- Provision of industrial development, house building and economic activities.
- The use of already developed areas, while making such areas attractive places to live and work.
- Conservation of the cultural and natural heritage.
- Development patterns which reduce the need to travel.

These objectives have now become part of planning orthodoxy and one would be hard pressed to find a local authority plan which does not couch its policies in these terms.

This emphasis on sustainable planning has been continued by Tony Blair's Labour Government. Upon assuming power, it produced a consultation paper, *Sustainable Development: Opportunities for Change*, in which it called for development which reduces harm to both people and environment. Development, it said, should encompass: social progress that recognizes everyone's needs; protection of the environment; prudent use of natural resources; and maintenance of economic growth. These aspirations were also to the fore in a *Better Quality of Life* published in 1999 which attempted to carry forward Labour's sustainable development objectives. Once again, the planning system was allocated a key role in ensuring that the various sustainability objectives (which although they may be contradictory) are reconciled.

In 1998 the new government produced *Planning for Sustainable Development: Towards Better Practice*. This document reiterated many of the points made in PPG 1 (indicating strong continuity between the governments of Major and Blair on key planning issues) and proposed that 'sustainable planning' should:

- Lead to development in existing urban areas in order to reduce the need to travel, diminish pressure on the countryside, and regenerate urban centres.
- Adopt a 'sequential approach' to development so that housing densities are raised and mixed uses are promoted (more controversially, this may also include new settlements and urban extensions).
- Increase the viability of market towns and villages at the same time as conserving the character of the countryside.
- Incorporate other key sustainability issues into planning decisions, such as climate change considerations (e.g. minimizing energy use), improving quality of air, soil and water, and conserving biodiversity.

A quick comparison of the two lists above shows that Conservative and Labour governments had moved to a consensus on the meaning of 'sustainable planning', with both placing considerable emphasis on urban regeneration and the concentration of development (this consensus is perhaps no coincidence as both were faced with the same problem of providing for development - notably new houses - in a context of environmental constraint - see Chapter 4 below). The main difference between the two approaches is that Labour placed more emphasis on the 'social' dimension of sustainability.

The emergence of the sustainability discourse during the 1990s bolstered the whole notion of environmental planning and gave rise to a new concern for environmental capacity and the capability of particular areas to withstand given levels of development (Rydin, 1998). Rather than simply delivering development, the planning system has therefore been forced to assess how it simultaneously delivers environmental goods and benefits (Blowers and Evans, 1997). This concern seems to hold the potential to 'embed' plans and planning in the complex ecologies of given territories (whether regions or localities) in which the natural, the economic and the social become profoundly intermeshed (Selman, 2000). Rather than thinking in uniform terms about given levels of development, planning policy must now take into account the spatial and environmental impacts of development.

We might assume, then, that the growing centrality of a more holistic environmental approach, encoded within a policy discourse around 'sustainable development', is leading to the emergence of a new kind of planning, one much more deeply committed to the preservation of environmental resources (on the scope for environmental planning within the land use planning system see Owens, 1994). However, we need to exercise caution here, for many commentators have pointed out that the continuities in planning are more striking than the changes. For instance, Elson *et al.* (1998), in a survey for the Rural Development Commission of PPGs, regional guidance, structure plans and local plans, find that in practice planners and planning authorities are employing very narrow understandings of 'sustainable development'. They say:

> [Sustainable development] is often taken simply to mean environmental protection and reducing travel needs by concentrating development into larger settlements. Those strands of sustainable development relating to economic development and social equity tend to be overlooked. Many local authorities view the government's planning policy guidance note (PPG 13 on Transport) as marking a shift towards concentrating development into larger settlements and, as their plans are revised policies... are becoming more restrictive (1998 p.4).

It is easy to see that, interpreted in this way, sustainable development fits in well with long standing planning policies and may in fact have bolstered the forces of preservationism and protectionism. This is certainly Cullingworth's (1997b p.948) view:

> [The concern for environment] has resulted in an alliance of old-style preservationists, concerned with local issues of environmental defence, and new-style environmentalists, concerned with wider issues of environmental quality and 'sustainability'...These are powerful forces, as the Conservative government discovered when it attempted, in the mid-1980s, to foster a more market-led planning policy in outer suburbia.

So how should we assess the new sustainable development agenda? Does it provide a new rationality for planning or is it simply an excuse for the continuation of old, well established policies? There may be something in both these views and the two positions may be reconcilable. In what follows we propose that the discourse of sustainability, while building on long-standing principles within the planning system, meshes with the move to re-spatialize planning policy, leading to the assertion of a new planning rationality. While this new rationality may only be emerging incrementally, and may be closely related to long established policy dispositions in planning (see Hall *et al.*, 1973), it is nevertheless congealing around a whole host of inter-linked concerns. For instance, in examining the debate around the housing projections, it is clear that opposition to the figures aims to bring them 'down to earth' by recontextualizing them within a complex set of environmental considerations. This is most explicit when the demands enshrined in the housing projections are assessed against calculations of environmental capacity (or 'capability') (Rydin, 1998). The spatialization trend is exacerbated by the use of sustainable development approaches, for they enhance the profile of environmental factors and allow these to be set against demands for new development. Spatial complexity thus replaces abstraction in planning's dominant mode of ordering.

Public participation and the assertion of spatiality

Another trend in contemporary planning that is helping to 'spatialize' policy is the encouragement of public participation. While this is a long-standing aspect of plan formulation and implementation (Pratchett, 1999), it has grown in importance, in part following the emergence of the environmental movement. On the one hand, environmentalism has encouraged the rise of direct action campaigns against road building and airport extensions (North, 1998; Wall, 1999), through the efforts of activists to push for a broad, societal set of changes in our behaviour towards nature. On the other hand, there has been an increase in more traditional forms of participation, oriented towards environmental policy change. Local politics of this type has been given particular emphasis in sustainable development policy, through, for instance, Local Agenda 21 initiatives (Buckingham-Hatfield and Percy, 1999; Mason, 1999; Young, 2000; Warburton, 1998). The emergence of this second type of environmental participation has led some commentators to argue that planning for sustainable development requires more participatory ways of working (Bishop, 2000).

As Yvonne Rydin (1999 p.84) has recently pointed out, public participation has been a consistent pre-occupation of the planning system: 'is there enough, is it the right sort, has sufficient account been taken of it?'. With the introduction of a comprehensive system of land use regulation in the 1947 Town and Country Planning Act, attention came to be focused on the democratic accountability of planners as they make decisions about the economic and social utilization of land. While elected councillors in local government provide a (limited) form of democratic overview, there has been a continuing concern that the public is being excluded from planning processes, both in terms of the formulation of development plans and in decisions around particular developments (which are presumed to be made in the light of the plan). As proposed by the Skeffington Committee, which was established by central government in the late 1960s in order to examine the whole issue of public participation, ideally planning should allow the public to 'share' in the formulation of policy and proposals (see Rydin, 1999 pp. 85-87). This concern to give the public their 'share' of policy space and time has been a recurring theme in planning policy, and public participation has come to be seen as 'an essential element in devolving more planning work down to the local government level, while maintaining support for planning decisions' (*Ibid.*, p. 85).

However, despite the attention it has received, public participation in planning has often been difficult to orchestrate. The complex structure of policy, in particular the two tier system of local planning, causes confusion amongst members of the public (Rydin, 1999), and 'outsiders' find it hard to know exactly when their efforts are required and when they are not. Moreover, the administrative boundaries used by planners do not always accord with local perceptions of community and locality, so that people often fail to recognize the community interest in development plans (Rydin, 1999). And even when they do become involved, members of the public often find the rather arcane and technical language of planning policy difficult to fathom. Moreover, successive government attempts to speed up plan making processes have usually worked against genuine public involvement.

Nevertheless, local environmental and community activists have for some time now been heavily involved in planning processes, and have sought to influence both decisions around specific developments (c.f. Murdoch and Marsden, 1995) and the formulation of development plans (Hull and Vigar, 1996; Murdoch *et al.*, 1999). With the shift to the plan-led system, and the requirement that development plans involve the public in the elaboration of policies, more structured participatory arenas came into being. As Vigar *et al.* comment (2000 p.15), 'it was certainly the case that during the 1990s, the attention given by stakeholders to involvement in development plan preparation increased substantially'. Thus, development plan reviews often incorporate wide-ranging debates about territorial development patterns. Hull (2000 p.772) notes that 'development plan consultation exercises have now become sites for discursive struggle with the average local plan receiving 1400 objections'. As many of these participants will seek to assert the natural and social value of their localities, we would expect participation to exacerbate the shift towards sustainable planning, that is, planning that genuinely weighs economic, social and environmental considerations against each other.

Encouragement of participation has also been an important concern for the Labour administration. The desire to 'modernize' local government led the new government to highlight issues of 'inclusion'. As Hull (2000 p.770) comments, the 'modernization' agenda has encouraged local authorities to 'demonstrate their commitment to individuals as citizens through public accountability and openness and through the involvement of user groups to advise and influence decision-making'. The implications for plan making are spelled out in PPG 12 (*Development Plans*) published in 1999. It states that:

> Local people and other interested bodies should have the opportunity to express their views on plan proposals before those proposals are finalized. The aim should be to encourage local people to participate actively in the preparation of plans from the early stages so they can be fully involved in decision about the pattern of development in their area. Consultation with the general public, community groups, conservation and amenity groups, business, development and infrastructure interests helps local plan authorities to secure a degree of consensus over the future development and use of land in their area.

Thus, while the Labour government seems to be downplaying the difficulties local authorities can face in achieving 'consensus', it is legitimizing extensive participatory activity at the local tier. Despite this policy emphasis, however, we should perhaps be careful not to exaggerate the current significance of participation. As we shall emphasize in subsequent chapters, participation at the local level is often constrained by policy making at the central level (a particular problem in the planning for housing sector). As Vigar *et al.* (2000 p.266) point out in their study of three English structure plans:

> the arenas of plan consultation and inquiry were highly constrained in their form and not readily accessible without considerable resources of knowledge and time...Those "voices" that did get heard then faced a policy agenda which was already well-defined and therefore difficult to challenge except at the level of specific projects. It was also set within the limits defined by the national Planning Policy Guidance Notes. This confined discussion to the "land use" dimensions of issues, assessed in the framework of nationally developed criteria. This detached the discussion from a developmental consideration of strategic policies for managing territories and locales.

The authors thus conclude that the potential of development plans to build up governance capacities at the local level, leading to an enhanced ability to assert territorial particularities in the policy process, has not so far been realized. We take up this point in subsequent chapters and provide further evidence of development plans failing in this regard. However, it is our view, to be outlined in the final chapter, that were plans to properly play this role, they would further strengthen the rationality of planning for sustainable development. To the extent that it is effective, participation tends to strengthen the rationality of 'sustainable' or 'spatial' development.

The impact of counterurbanization

Local level participatory activity has been particularly noticeable in the rural areas of the UK (Abram *et al.*, 1996; Murdoch and Marsden, 1994). While concern for the countryside can be attributed to a generalized increase in environmental awareness, it also, in part, stems from a rather fundamental shift in the nature of the rural population, with increasing numbers of rural dwellers now taking a particular interest in protection of the natural environment (Hall *et al.*, 1973; Short *et al.*, 1986; Murdoch and Marsden, 1994; Boyle and Halfacree, 1998). This shift, which is usually referred to as 'counterurbanization' (Champion, 1994), has raised the profile of the community interest in planning. It has also given participation a particularly rural flavour, so that the concerns of rural dwellers are frequently voiced particularly forcefully in plan review processes (see chapters 5 and 6). In our view, this process underpins the shift in planning's prevailing rationalities.

According to Champion (1994 p.1504), counterurbanization really became a noticeable phenomenon between 1961 and 1971, when metropolitan growth in the UK was virtually static but the rural population - for the first time since industrialization - began to increase. Between 1971 and 1981 this trend continued,

Table 2.1   Population change for largely rural districts (1981-91%)

	Total	Natural	Migration
Great Britain	+7.6	-0.6	+8.6
East Anglia	+11.0	-0.4	+11.4
South West	+9.9	-0.7	+10.6
Yorks & Humbs	+8.5	-0.7	+9.3
West Midlands	+7.1	-0.8	+7.9
East Midlands	+6.8	-0.3	+7.1
South East	+6.0	+0.9	+5.1
Wales	+5.4	-0.9	+6.3
Northern	+4.6	-3.0	+7.6
Scotland	+4.0	-0.2	+4.2

Note no districts of this type exist in the North West region.
Source: Champion, 1994 p.1513.

Table 2.2   Net migration changes in English counties (1981-91 %)

Counties Gaining Population		Counties Losing Population	
Dorset	+11.8	S. Yorks	-5.1
Isle of Wight	+10.3	Tyne & Wear	-5.7
Cornwall	+10.2	Gt. Mancs	-7.3
E. Sussex	+9.1	Cleveland	-8.2
Somerset	+8.3	Gt. London	-8.5
W. Sussex	+7.8	W. Midlands	-8.7
Devon	+7.3	Merseyside	-10.3
Norfolk	+6.8		
Cambs	+6.5		
W. Yorks	+5.9		
Lincs	+5.6		
Shropshire	+5.5		

Source: Halliday and Coombes, 1995 p.435.

with metropolitan areas losing 2.3 per cent of their population while non-metropolitan areas increased their share by 6.0 per cent (with rural areas increasing their population by an astonishing 9.4 per cent). The 1971 to 1981 census showed clear evidence that the fastest growing places were small towns and remote rural areas (Champion and Townsend, 1990). Although the population of metropolitan Britain began to grow again between 1981 and 1991, the free-standing small towns and rural regions increased their total residents by 6.0 per cent (see Champion, 1994).

The examination of more detailed figures shows further evidence of rural growth during the 1980s and Champion (1994 p.1513) concludes that population growth and net in-migration were relatively widespread across rural Britain over this decade (see Table 2.1).If these figures are disaggregated to the county level we can see clearly that the more rural counties gain population at a time when the more urban counties are losing population. The figures in Table 2.2 show that the most 'rural' counties gained population, while the older industrial areas tended to lose numbers. However, the table is pitched at a spatial scale that covers both urban and rural residential areas. A little more clarity can be gained from data referring to individual local authority districts. Only seven of the 102 districts in the remote, largely rural category experienced population decline during the 1981-91 period (these were primarily located in the most remote areas of Scotland). Thus, the central point to emerge from the 1991 census was that rural Britain experienced population growth during the 1980s due to in-migration, with the strongest percentage gainers in population being some of the remotest rural areas in counties such as Devon, Dorset, Cornwall, Lincolnshire and Somerset. All metropolitan areas - with the exception of London, which managed to retain its population share - lost population during the same period.

Evidence collected since the last census by Champion (1996) and Champion *et al.* (1998) seems to indicate that these trends proceed apace, with the metropolitan areas continuing to lose population. Thus, Champion (1996 p.14) argues that 'each level of the hierarchy receives net in-migration from all higher levels and dispatches net out-migration to all lower levels in the manner of a full-scale "cascade", or indeed "general downpour"'. This cascade is the essential component of counterurbanization and the message is clear: counterurbanization continues (see also Dorling, 1995).

In turning to examine the forces that lie behind counterurbanization, we can begin by identifying some of the most generally recognized causes of population movement. Coleman and Salt (1992 p.401) argue that it is possible to divide the mobile English into two main groupings. Firstly, there are those whose residential moves are associated with life cycle changes. Such changes tend to conform to a general pattern: young people move to the cities to enjoy the 'bright lights', retreat to the suburbs or smaller towns when they marry and have children, and then gravitate to more peripheral rural areas or seaside resorts as retirement looms. The second grouping refers to those whose moves are dominated by career considerations. Career migration is linked to the occupational characteristics of migrants such as education level, skill, income, nature of employment etc. and as individuals proceed from job to job so a geographical pattern of mobility will occur. These features of migration are not new. What is new, however, is the scale of the shift away from large urban centres to small rural settlements. This seems to indicate that both the lifestyle and career forms of migration are being fashioned around *rural* moves. More than ever, disillusionment with the conurbations and the yearning for a rural life are governing migration decisions.

Thus Fielding (1990 p.230) proposes that counterurbanization is being driven by some form of 'anti-urbanism', one which 'characterize[s] cities as the sites of stress and conflict, and the countryside as the realm of harmony and sociability'. With increases in private affluence, associated with private car ownership and improved rail and road communication links, comes the opportunity for those with the impetus to move to their most favoured countryside locations to do so (Cross, 1990).

From the various studies conducted into the counterurbanization phenomenon (e.g. Bell, 1994; Murdoch and Marsden, 1994; Boyle and Halfacree, 1998; Halfacree, 1994), it is possible to conclude, in general terms, that the movement of residents into rural areas reflects a desire for two things: firstly, a particular kind of *material* environment, one that is aesthetically pleasing with traditional buildings, open space, countryside etc. and, secondly, a particular *social* environment which includes being part of village life and a rural community, having a sense of belonging and so on. Often these two aspects become closely aligned with one another. As Howard Newby (1985 p.23) puts it:

> Ideas about the English countryside as a visual phenomenon and ideas about the countryside as a social phenomenon have... merged together. A locality which looks right must also, it is assumed, support a desirable way of life. In this way, rural aesthetics and ideas about rural society have become closely intertwined.

According to Bell (1994), the security of the country identity derives from 'pastoralism', that is, proximity to nature. The significance of pastoralism lies in the counterurbanizer's belief that nature is 'free from social interests', it is 'something that stands apart from the selfishness, greed, power, and domination they see in social [that is, urban] life' (1994 p.138). consequently, he argues that through an affiliation with the countryside, counterurbanizers hope to gain a secure moral foundation for their lives. In his study of a village in south-east England during the early 1990s, Bell provides an elaborate extension of the idea that people are moving into rural areas in order to escape the 'rat race'. He finds that what the villagers share is a desire to see in the countryside a natural realm which exists *outside* the strict utilitarian economic principles which structure their everyday lives. Thus, in accessible rural areas, affluent newcomers, whose daily working lives are governed in many cases by highly pressurized jobs, seek out residential spaces which allow some form of 'escape'. Village life offers the most obvious 'escape route' from the demanding economic world that many middle-class people now find themselves working in.

There are, of course, certain ironies here which are noted by Charlesworth and Cochrane (1994) in their study of rural areas in south-east England. They argue that though counterurbanizers are seeking out 'peace and quiet' in the countryside, their economic status (and perhaps their ability to live in affluent areas at all) depends upon being part and parcel of the extremely dynamic economy of the south-east region. Yet this economy also threatens the countryside, for levels of development seem to extend further and further from urban cores. As the regional economy grows so the protection of the countryside becomes a more urgent task and rural residents have to expend a great deal of energy in order to ensure that it remains free from undesirable forms of development (Abram *et al.*, 1996; Cloke and Little, 1990; Murdoch and Marsden, 1994; Short *et al.*, 1986; Savage *et al.*, 1992).

For counterurbanizers, protection of the countryside is achieved first and foremost through planning (Lowe, 1977). Thus, enhanced scope for participation in plan making processes will be utilized by counterurbanizing groups as they attempt to protect their rural spaces from further development. Moreover, it is likely that engaging in participatory activities will further enhance the attachment of local residents to the countryside: the more rural areas are threatened, the more valuable they become. Thus, the planning system will be extensively utilized in order to protect rural communities and natural environments. In short the new counterurbanizers are likely to provide a powerful impetus behind planning for sustainable development. Planning policies that strengthen the protectionist aspect of planning will be especially welcome to this social formation. Moreover, counterurbanizing groups in the south of England tend to be politically influential, as they showed firstly in the mid- to late-1980s, when Mrs Thatcher's government attempted to loosen planning controls, and again in the mid-1990s, when John Major's government proposed that extensive new housing developments might be required.

In the mid-1990s, with housing forecasts predicting 4.4 million homes would be needed to meet likely demand, the forces of protectionism were mobilized. For instance, *Country Life*, a magazine aimed at the more 'establishment' sectors of both those who live in and enjoy access to the countryside, asks on the cover of its November 13th 1997 issue: 'how many new houses will swamp the countryside you love?'. The same edition also highlights the fears which surround increasing patterns of house building and migration in the countryside in its leader column. It said:

> Anyone who keeps his or her eyes open, travelling round, say, the Shire counties, will realize the damage that has been wrought in recent decades. Villages where everyone used to know each other have become unrecognizable to their older inhabitants. With the new development have come more roads, more street lights, more water extraction - and in this age of car-ownership, village shops and schools continue to close. Yet the

countryside is an immeasurably great asset for these islands. It has become the focus of our identity. We cannot afford to lose more.

The new rural residents could thus claim that, in the wake of the 4.4 million forecast, the countryside was 'under siege' (as the same edition of the magazine puts it). This constituency was thus ready to put pressure on the new Labour administration to diminish the impacts of new housing on rural areas. And we should not assume that its political influence will be lost on a Labour government: as we shall see, many of the most significant policy innovations made by Labour in the planning field have been as a result of exactly the same political pressures faced by Margaret Thatcher and John Major.

Conclusion

As this chapter has shown, planning policy has been through a variety of twists and turns in recent years. We find efforts to liberalize the system, thereby making it more responsive to development needs, running up against political resistance, and this resistance is most forcefully expressed in the rural areas of southern England where large numbers of new residents are seeking to protect the natural environment and rural communities. A political constituency, oriented to 'grounding' planning in local environmental conditions has therefore emerged during 1980s and 1990s. Mrs Thatcher fell foul of this constituency and John Major subsequently set about repairing the damage. In seeking to placate Conservative voters in southern England, Major's government made planning stronger. In so doing, it enhanced the environmental aspects, especially after 'sustainable development' was adopted as a goal of policy. As this new policy goal has worked its way through the planning framework so it has begun to recast planning's spatial sensitivity.

In concluding this chapter, we should, however, add a cautionary note: despite the growing significance of spatial thinking and environmentalism, planning cannot only be concerned only with protection. As Healey and Shaw (1994 p.426) put it:

> the planning system seems to provide a flexible regulatory regime... a set of formal mechanisms and practices built up around them through which the tensions between the potentially conflicting objectives of economic development, meeting social demands and needs and conserving and enhancing environmental quality may be managed.

Protection, preservation, and planning for sustainable development are not the whole story. Planning facilitates development at the same time as it provides arenas for the expression of environmental concern. Two rationalities of planning appear to co-exist, with the emphasis on each changing over time. Thus, planning frequently finds itself caught between the two discourses of 'development' and 'environment'. Nowhere is this more evident than in planning for housing. The planning system is committed to ensuring that sufficient housing is built to meet economic and social demands. For many years it has done this quite successfully, so that owner-occupied housing has grown considerably in the post war period (see Savage *et al.*, 1993). Yet counterurbanization, as well as increased public participation and policy concerns for 'sustainable development', have ensured that there is now great opposition to housing development and the tensions running through planning for housing grew during the whole period under review here.

When John Major vacated Downing Street he left behind a fear that the countryside was about to be 'swamped' (in that felicitous phrase first made famous, in quite another context, by Mrs Thatcher) by a wave of new housing. Dealing with this fear became an unexpectedly pressing problem for Tony Blair's government (especially in the wake of the Countryside Marches which seemed to capture a feeling that Labour was 'out of touch' with the countryside). In seeking to diffuse this issue, the Environment Secretary, John Prescott, broadly continued the Majorite approach (Allmendinger and Tewdwr-Jones, 2000): he attempted, on the one hand, to promote an 'urban renaissance' (in order to diminish pressure for new housing in the countryside) and, on the other hand, sought to restructure the responsibilities allocated to the various tiers of government. While it is still a little early to pass judgement on this policy, we can recognize that it has not been easy to introduce, partly because the two rationalities of 'development' and 'environment' seem to uneasily co-exist within the policy (Murdoch, 2000).

In the next few chapters we assess the implications of the trends discussed above. We show that while the spatial rationality is firmly on the planning agenda, it currently sits within a governmental structure that has traditionally functioned to ensure the local delivery of (housing) development. We thus consider whether a restructuring of responsibilities within the state (driven by the need to expand territorial discretion) will ultimately succeed in diminishing opposition to planning for housing in the south east of England. In order to build up this assessment we must firstly outline how responsibilities have traditionally been distributed between the state agencies responsible for the formulation and implementation of planning policy. We need to show the effects of this distribution on the nature and conduct of the policy process. In Chapter 3 we examine general planning policy at the national, regional and local scales. In Chapter 4 we look specifically at planning for housing in order to examine how the dispute between development and environment has been managed in this sector. In chapters 5 and 6 we consider the way policy affects those local areas that are set to receive new housing. In particular, we focus upon the way local activists run up against a dominant 'discursive line' (Jessop, 1998; Murdoch and Abram, 1998) when opposing new housing development. This line effectively constructs a 'line of force' across the planning for housing field and draws alliances between technologies, government agencies, developers and local planners. We look at how resistance to this line is couched in a discourse of spatial complexity and sustainable development and show that this discourse, likewise, enables alliances to be established across the governmental domain. In Chapter 7 we turn to consider in more detail the impact of recent reforms and ask whether the fierce debates that have run through planning for housing are heralding the emergence of a new planning rationality, one that privileges one set of discursive repertoires over others.

Chapter 3

The Policy Hierarchy in Planning

Introduction

As we saw in the previous chapter, the Conservative governments of the 1980s enhanced the status of developmentalism in planning. They sought to ensure that this rationality was enacted within a hierarchical structure of government in which policy is elaborated centrally and then disseminated throughout the policy framework. In refining this framework, Mrs Thatcher's governments attempted to *centralize* policy making (in a small number of agencies located in Whitehall) through greater central state involvement in directing the implementation of policy) and to *decentralize* policy delivery (so that both sate and non-state actors worked in partnership). These changes - which are usually summarized under the heading of 'governance' (Stoker, 1998b; 2000) - forced local authorities to 'deliver' centrally formulated policies.

However, while the shift to a 'governance' system certainly affected the governmental context in which planning was conducted, it is questionable how far it altered the nature of planning practice and policy. Commentators such as Cullingworth (1997 a and b) believe that, in attempting to reform the system to better entrench the 'market' ethos, the Conservatives ran up against protectionist forces in their electoral heartland (forces which, as we saw in the last chapter, were gradually growing stronger during this period). John Major's government responded by introducing legislation that actually strengthened planning's traditional role. This legislation gave a higher status to development plans and enhanced processes of participation. It also legitimized 'sustainable development' as a policy goal. While these innovations can be seen as broadly in line with those protectionist strands that have long run through planning policy (see Hall *et al.*, 1973; Cullingworth, 1997b), we believe that they have now consolidated in a new rationality or 'mode of ordering'.

Others, however, have counselled caution in proposing such an interpretation. Allmendinger and Tewdwr-Jones (1997), for instance, argue that while development plans may have been given an enhanced status in the early 1990s, the significance of this is easily overestimated. They point to a coterminous strengthening of national policy (see also Vigar *et al.*, 2000). So, while many planning practitioners and participants might *think* that a plan-led system has been introduced (with all the significance that holds for the spatialization of planning),

43

and may *act* as though such a policy is meaningful, we should not be so easily taken in. In the view of these authors, the central state still holds the reins of power in the planning policy framework.

Such competing interpretations force us to ask the following question: where does planning policy come from? Does it emerge from a central authority which directs all the various parts of the system or does it emanate from the interaction of a whole multitude of authorities located at different tiers, scales and places? In other words, is planning policy a *single* policy, which is applied uniformly across all parts of the system, or is it the *aggregation* of different policies or differing interpretations of policy? We consider these questions here because, in trying to answer them, we can sketch in a little more clearly the context within which the new rationality of environmentalism is emerging and can ask whether a structure that was designed to deliver 'development' is capable of delivering 'sustainable development'.

First, we examine how the formulation of general planning policy is undertaken by the central state as it attempts to provide consistency in decision making across the system as a whole. It is often assumed that if local planning authorities are permitted to make all their own decisions in whatever way they see fit then there will be widely divergent planning outcomes in different places. Thus, national policy - as encoded, for instance, in the planning policy guidance notes - attempts to provide some co-ordination in decision making. We must ask, then, what is the relationship between this general policy and local decision making? Does central planning policy 'determine' what goes on in regional and local planning authorities (as Allmendinger and Tewdwr-Jones, 1997, appear to argue) or is the policy merely a form of 'guidance' which regional and local authorities must interpret in line with their own particular circumstances?

After considering the policy-making role of the central state we turn to examine the role of the region in the planning policy hierarchy. As we shall see, the region has traditionally been the weakest of the planning policy tiers; its powers have been squeezed by a central state keen to retain overall responsibility for policy making and a local state keen to retain control of implementation. Yet, this situation is changing, as the regional state is gradually gaining an enhanced status in the policy framework. Having outlined the new powers of the regions, we then go on to examine the local state and consider whether 'local discretion', which is often seen as the defining characteristic of the English planning system, remains in place. We argue that, following the shift to a plan-led system, this issue has gained even more significance.

Running through this chapter, then, is a consideration of 'governance' in planning. Our interest in this topic stems from a need to understand how well the planning policy structure can accommodate the rationality of 'planning for sustainable development'. Or, to put it another way, we need to ask how much scope there is for the assertion of 'territorial' or 'spatial' concerns in the current hierarchy. Is planning dominated by abstract uniform policy principles or does it have the capability to respond to diverse socio-spatial formations? In addressing these issues, we show that while planning appears to emerge from a strict governmental hierarchy - thereby constraining any move to a genuinely multi-level system - there is some amount of discretion at each stage of the policy tier. This discretion is used in differing ways by differing authorities. Its use is also the subject of continual negotiation between the tiers themselves. Discretion, however, varies between sectors. Thus, in the next chapter we look in more detail at how the central state has attempted to constrain discretion in the planning for housing sector while in subsequent chapters we show how this attempt has resulted in a constant struggle to assert a 'strategic line' in the face of territorially-based resistance.

Central government policy

Central government responsibility for planning lies with the DETR, a department that has been through many changes since it was established in 1971, including most recently the incorporation of transport into its remit. Effectively, the DETR sets out broad planning policies, although the Secretary of State for the Environment has extensive formal powers in relation to the planning system. These, in effect, give the DETR the final say in policy matters (such as the composition of Use Class Orders and General Development Orders) and the Secretary of State has the power to 'call in' plans or development control decisions which are seen to substantially diverge from national policy. When conflict emerges between central and local government (such as over housing numbers or the composition of local plans) the Secretary of State becomes the final arbiter. The planning component of DETR comprises seven divisions which advise ministers on land use planning issues. Its main areas of work include the holding of local plan inquiries, determining planning appeals and enforcement orders (Cullingworth and Nadin, 1997). Also important at the central level is the Planning Inspectorate, which serves both DETR and the Welsh Office. This is an executive agency within the nest of organizations that determine planning policy at the central level.

Central government's main role is to 'co-ordinate the work of individual local authorities and to ensure that their development plans and development control procedures are in harmony with broad planning policies' (Cullingworth and Nadin, 1997 p.47). Planning authorities, inspectors and the other actors involved in planning practice are 'guided in their decisions by government policy' (*ibid.*). Since the late 1980s, policy has come primarily in the form of the PPGs. According to Quinn (1996), these guidance notes perform two main functions: they ensure that national concerns are pursued at the local level and they promote consistency and quality in local decision making. They aim to ensure that all policy levels 'interlock as far as possible into a coherent whole' (Wilson, 1990, quoted in Tewdwr-Jones, 1997 p.145).

In the context of the 'plan-led' system - which was heralded by the legislative changes of the early 1990s (discussed in the last chapter) - PPG policies make themselves felt primarily through the development plan system: as Quinn

(1996. p.19) puts it, 'national guidance has no statutory role in individual decisions beyond its influence on the development plan' (with an added presumption that plans must, as far as possible, incorporate the very latest Government guidance), although he also notes that PPGs have developed a strong role in law, as the Courts have tended to uphold a view that government statements of planning policy are 'material considerations' that must be taken into account in planning decisions (Tewdwr-Jones, 1994a). However, as the planning system requires 'that all cases be considered on their merits within the framework of relevant policies' (Cullingworth and Nadin, 1997 p.48), then the PPGs cannot be too prescriptive; they must leave room for the discretion that is thought to be so central to the system of land use planning in the UK.

In the context of PPGs, policies must be pitched at a rather general level so that they can be tailored to local circumstances. This can give rise to problems, however, as Quinn (1996 p. 25) notes:

> not all PPGs seem as clearly expressed as decision-takers might sometimes wish. PPGs are policy statements, with all the subtlety and balance that entails, but they are often examined at public enquiry with forensic zeal as if they were some form of contract. This is an examination that they often cannot stand.

The lack of clarity that Quinn sees as a necessary part of a balanced policy, is seen by others as a recipe for confusion and muddle. Trevor Roberts (1998), for instance, argues that PPGs should be scrapped. He says: 'they are a hopeless confusion of firm government policy; policy masquerading as advice; advice masquerading as policy; and advice which varies from the helpful to the confused and the contradictory'. For Quinn, (1996 p. 25) however, this confusion often arises because the guidance notes very properly express a number of complex objectives: 'it is the nature of planning for there always to be competing priorities to weigh in the balance and it is right that PPGs should set these out'.

According to Tewdwr-Jones (1994a), the provision of guidance to shape local policy and procedures is perhaps the most important trend in planning policy in recent years. As he points out, PPG 1 (*General Policy and Principles*) states (in both the 1992 and 1997 versions) that

> the Government's statements of planning policy are material considerations which must be taken into account, where relevant, in decisions on planning applications. These statements cannot make irrelevant any matter which is a material consideration in a particular case. But, where such statements indicate the weight that should be given to relevant considerations, decision makers must have proper regard to them. If they elect not to follow relevant statements of the Government's planning policy, they must give clear and convincing reasons (DoE, 1992/1997 para. 52).

Tewdwr-Jones (1994a) interprets this emphasis in policy as a 'check' on development plans. It seems likely, therefore, that in circumstances where a local plan and a policy diverge, it will be the plan which is brought back into line (especially as the Secretary of State can call in any 'inappropriate' plans for central adjudication). Tewdwr-Jones (1994a p.111) argues that, 'superficially' the plan (in the 'plan-led' system) has been given more weight in development control decision making, but this is consistently undermined by the requirement to line everything up with national policy (a requirement that is bolstered, he argues, by the literal interpretation of this policy by planning inspectors). Thus, Tewdwr-Jones discerns an inflexible approach emerging, one which constrains local decision making to an unwarranted degree (see also Vigar *et al.*, 2000).

To summarize, two sets of criticisms have been made of the policies encoded into PPGs: firstly, they are vague and confused and, secondly, they are constraining of local level decision making. Superficially, it might seem that these two criticisms are contradictory. However, Tewdwr-Jones (1994b pp. 587-588) brings them together by arguing that the PPG documents are failing to provide clear, accessible, systematic advice or guidance to decision makers, with the result that they also fail to 'provide the broad national framework for the formulation and implementation of policies at the lower levels of the hierarchy'. He believes that PPGs have become 'directives' which relate to detailed local development control issues but which do not take account of the broad economic and social contexts in which development control decisions are made. Moreover, they contain very detailed development control policies on some topics (e.g. telecommunications and archaeology) and very little on others (economic development and urban policy) (Tewdwr-Jones, 1997 p.148). As a consequence,

> local planning authorities, wishing to avoid lengthy policy battles with central government over the most contentious issues, are replicating [central government] policy in their plans with statements that are easily interpretive for any given situation, and are leaving the interpretation task to development control officers or supplementary planning guidance.

Despite such localized interpretation, however, Tewdwr-Jones concludes that government is 'utilizing the contents of PPGs...to secure consistency and continuity in the framing of planning policies' (1997 p.157). Thus, the 'policy structure operates too excessively from the top downwards, and there is very little opportunity for local conditions and factors to outweigh the guidance provided by higher tiers in the structure' (1994b p.592).

As part of his assessment of the PPG system, Tewdwr-Jones (1997) undertakes a survey of English and Welsh metropolitan and non-metropolitan districts and London boroughs to try to gain some insight into the way planning officers view the policy guidance system. On the whole, he finds satisfaction with the operation of the PPG/plan-led approach and is therefore forced to conclude that 'the use of PPGs in providing direction and monitoring in the plan-led process, although far from perfect, forms an important part of the operation of land use planning in England and Wales' (1997 p.161). Thus, while the system might be overly top-down in nature, it still seems to be performing some valuable functions. These functions were spelled out more clearly in an investigation of the effectiveness of PPGs by Land Use Consultants on behalf of the DoE in 1995. After undertaking a comprehensive survey of PPG users, the consultants (1995 pp.ii-iii) found that 'PPGs have assisted greatly in ensuring a more consistent approach to the formulation of development plan policies' while also continuing to take account 'of the discretionary powers of local authorities'. Thus, 'PPGs are a remarkably effective means of disseminating national planning policy priorities...'.

The commentaries referred to above all emerged during the period of John Major's government. We need now to make some reference to recent changes introduced by the Labour government since 1997. In *Modernizing Planning* (DETR, 1998a) the new government's first major policy document on the planning system, it was stated, in reference to national policy, that in some areas, i.e. those relating to particularly contentious and large scale developments such as motorways, rail links, airports, power stations and so on, policy needs to be more explicit, in part to cut down on the time taken at public inquiry. When *Planning* (the official magazine of the Royal Town Planning Institute) came to assess the Government's progress in January 1999 (see the January 15th edition), one year after the publication of *Modernizing Planning*, it was noted that sharper policy statements had been issued in the line with the above proposal, especially in the areas of housing and transport.

No mention was made in this policy statement about the existing national planning guidance notes so it was assumed that the new government was happy to continue with those inherited from its predecessor, at least for a limited period (Tewdwr-Jones, 1998). The subsequent publication of PPGs under Labour reinforces the perception that it is largely content to continue the policies of its predecessor (PPG 1 on *General Policies and Principles* remains in force despite being written during John Major's tenure). PPG 12 (*Development Plans*) published in 1999 states that:

> In preparing plans, local authorities must have regard to national policies set out in PPGs... However, authorities should not repeat large sections of such documents in plans. The emphasis should be on producing development plan policies which implement national and regional policy at the local level. Where the local authority intends to propose a policy in their plan which departs from guidance provided in a PPG or MPG [minerals policy guidance], they should ensure that they have adequate reasons for doing so. The Secretary of State may intervene in cases where a structure plan, UDP or local plan goes against national policy guidance without justifiable reasons being provided (DETR, 1999c para.11).

PPG 12 emphasizes that local authority planners must pay close attention to the PPGs when developing plan policies. In other words, the plan-led approach introduced by John Major's government continues with its essentials intact.

To conclude this section, and in answer to the question 'where does planning policy come from', it would appear as though policy emerges fairly unambiguously from the central state. Central government uses the PPGs to influence decisions down the planning hierarchy. The system allows shifts in policy to be quickly communicated to planning authorities and other actors involved in the system (partly because policy can be changed without reference to Parliament). In this sense, policy is 'top-down'.

However, we should perhaps not overstate this, for many commentators believe that discretion still lies at the heart of the planning system (Cullingworth and Nadin, 1997). PPGs are often very broad and even, at times, ambiguous so that local interpretation remains a key part of the implementation process. Thus, while the direction of policy comes from above, its implementation is strongly shaped from below. And if we examine policy in the round, in a way that includes both formulation and implementation, then we can say that general planning policy - as encoded in the PPGs - does emerge from an institutional system that has some similarities to governance systems: central government delivers policies which strongly 'enable' other institutions and actors in the system to concentrate upon delivery. Central government is in no position to deliver planning policy itself: it is heavily reliant on a host of other agencies (not least private developers). And these other agencies have some (limited?) scope to insert their own (territorial) concerns into planning policy.

Regional planning policy

The regional level has traditionally been the weakest tier of planning in the UK. Prior to devolution, special arrangements had been in existence for Scotland and Wales, with slightly differing structures of local government in each country. In terms of planning policy, the Scottish Office has long had the ability to prepare specifically Scottish policy guidance, while in Wales, the Welsh Office has similar powers of discretion, and has used them most often in relation to topics that have a distinctly Welsh flavour (e.g. Welsh language issues). Although planning policy in these two countries has often mirrored that found in England, the establishment of the Scottish Parliament and the Welsh Assembly would seem to herald a likely divergence in their respective planning policies (although Tanner, 2001, argues that recent planning guidance produced by the Welsh Assembly still fails to achieve this divergence in any significant respect).

The moves to strengthen regional planning in Wales and Scotland are mirrored to a much less significant extent in England (largely because few English people view the region as a meaningful source of identity - in a recent social attitudes survey only 15 per cent said they favoured regional devolution - see

Bogdanor, 2001). While local planning authorities have been co-operating at the regional level for many years now - the south east regional planning forum (SERPLAN), for instance, came into existence in 1962 - it is only over the last decade that central government has given any real encouragement to this activity. According to Baker (1998 p.154) 'the period from the late 1970s through to the early 1990s can be identified as almost totally barren in terms of regional and even strategic (sub-regional) planning policy in the UK'.

By the late 1980s, however, increasing concerns in the south of England about the inexorable spread of new housing development - discussed in Chapter 2 - led to pressure for some degree of strategic planning (Baker *et al.*, 1999). This move had already been presaged in the 1986 consultation paper, *The Future of Development Plans*, which cited with some approval the progress that has been made in certain regions, such as East Anglia and the West Midlands, in producing regional strategies to guide the decisions of local authorities. The consultation paper proposed that the Secretary of State should begin to issue guidance to the regional planning fora so that the regions could be more explicitly linked into a national structure. However, it was emphasized that the regional bodies would not be formalized into statutory bodies, as this would have implications for the power of local authorities. Moreover, neither the DoE (Department of Environment, as the DETR was previously known) nor the Welsh Office wished to see the regional planning system develop into a more effective form of regional planning; they wished to keep it very much as an advisory system (Alden and Offord, 1996).

The 1989 White Paper *The Future of Development Plans*, however, gave some encouragement to the production of regional guidance and PPG 15, produced in 1990, stated that 'the aim should be to have guidance in place for most regions during the early 1990s' (quoted in Baker, 1998 p.155). Under these arrangements, 'conferences' of local planning authorities - mainly county councils, but also including district and national park authorities - were to produce advice to the Secretary of State in the form of draft guidance. The Secretary of State would then take this into account when publishing regional planning guidance (initially regional guidance was published as part of the PPG series but a separate regional planning guidance - RPG - series was established in 1989). Thus the local authorities would do most of the preparatory work on regional guidance but the final policy decisions were to be taken by central government.

With the introduction of the plan led system following the 1991 Act, it was emphasized that the primary function of regional guidance is to provide the necessary framework for the preparation of structure plans. Section 2 of PPG 12, published in 1992, covered the preparation, content timing and progress of regional planning guidance and made the following points:

- Regional guidance will normally cover those issues that are of regional importance or that need to be considered on a wider basis than structure plans.
- Regional planning guidance will be limited to matters relevant to development plans.
- Topics covered depend on circumstances in each region.
- Guidance will suggest a development framework for a period of twenty years.
- It will cover priorities for environment, transport, economic development, agriculture, minerals, waste and infrastructure.

Regional planning guidance was subsequently produced in all regions of England. Standing conferences also came into being (to be replaced subsequently by regional assemblies), and these bodies took on the responsibility for the future revision of regional guidance.

According to Baker (1998), although RPG is not yet a statutory part of the planning system, its status and importance has grown since the early 1990s. Various reasons are adduced for this. For instance, institutional innovations elsewhere in government, notably the establishment of Government Offices for the Regions by John Major's government, have prompted a growth in regional planning. These Offices initiated greater co-ordination between regional actors and there was a need for a regional planning presence in this context (John and Whitehead, 1997). The main impetus for regional planning, however, was recognition that many planning policy concerns can only be adequately addressed at a wider scale than that of local development plans:

> The quest for sustainable development patterns; the role of green belts; the impact of large out-of-town employment and retail centres; the relationship between metropolitan areas and their hinterlands; and meeting future housing needs all involve planning policy considerations which cross existing administrative boundaries. These can only be addressed by an effective regional planning framework... (Baker, 1998 p.165).

With the election of the Labour Government in 1997 the trend towards stronger regional planning continued. While the most important innovation was undoubtedly the introduction of elected bodies in Scotland and Wales, the introduction of Regional Development Agencies (RDAs) in England was also significant. It was intended that the RDAs would promote economic development and regeneration, investment and competitiveness, employment, skills and educational development and, lastly, sustainable development (DETR, 1997). The RDAs were to take on some of the functions of Government Offices and regional quangos. However, the government made it clear that the new RDAs would not take any powers away from local government. Thus, land use planning was excluded from the RDA remit; it was to remain under local democratic control. While the relation between the two sets of institutions was not clearly defined at this time, hopes were expressed that they would be 'parallel and complementary' (Johnston, 1998). It is not surprising, then, that the introduction of these agencies put the issue of a statutory planning tier more squarely on the governmental agenda, especially as some regional planning authorities believe:

> there needs to be much greater clarity about the relationship between regional planning guidance and the strategies of the RDAs. Without such clarity, and under the current institutional arrangements, there will be no means of resolving any tensions that arise between the two types of strategies (SERPLAN, 1999a p.1).

Thus far, however, any strengthening of regional planning has been gradual. In 1998 the Government published a consultation paper entitled the *Future of Regional Planning Guidance*. The paper began by stating that 'the interests of the English regions have been neglected in recent years and this government intends to reverse that neglect'. It proposed that there are two ways of achieving this: one is via the RDAs; the other is 'by improving the arrangements for co-ordination of land use, transport and economic development planning at the regional level'. The document recognizes that regional planning has been limited in its effectiveness and gives the following reasons:

- Regional guidance has too often lacked regional focus and has spent too much time reiterating national policies.
- The system is narrow and land use oriented.
- Guidance lacks sufficient environmental objectives and has few appraisal mechanisms.
- It does not command commitment from regional stakeholders, partly because the process of producing it is insufficiently transparent.

The consultation paper sets out to address these issues. It proposed that the regional planning conference should have more responsibility for actually producing the guidance so that it can better reflect regional rather than national priorities. The conference will therefore work closely with regional stakeholders, allowing the production of a more representative product. It is also suggested that the guidance be subject to an examination-in-public in order to make the various issues more transparent. However, it is argued that the scope of RPG should be effectively confined to land use planning issues, leaving economic development issues to the new RDAs.

These various aspirations emerged in the new approach to regional planning outlined in PPG 11, published in 1999. The PPG stresses that it:

places greater responsibility on regional planning bodies, working with Government Offices and regional stakeholders, to resolve planning issues at the regional level through the production of draft RPG. This will promote greater local ownership of regional policies and increased commitment to their implementation through the statutory planning process (DETR, 1999b p.3).

The guidance note sets out the new arrangements for RPG preparation and emphasizes the potential for policy development at the regional level. It proposes that RPG should:

- Provide a concise spatial or physical development strategy.
- Address regional or sub-regional issues and take advantage of the range of development options that exist at that level.
- Link policy objectives to priorities, targets and indicators so that the strategy can be monitored and reviewed.
- Be specific to the region so that, while it should refer to national policies, it should 'not simply repeat them nor resort to platitudes'.
- Be location- but not site- specific i.e. regional planning should not descend into the level of detail more appropriate to a development plan.

The PPG says that regional planning should now emerge from a process of collaboration in which a range of 'stakeholders' articulates a planning approach tailored to the needs of the region.

Concerns remain, however, that despite this emphasis on 'collaboration', no clear framework exists to bind together the various regional strategies now emerging. This concern is most acute over the relationship between the regional economic strategies produced by the RDAs and RPG produced by the regional planning body (RPB). A number of commentators have proposed that in the absence of a 'hierarchy' of strategies, economic development interests will dominate those concerned with planning (Murdoch and Tewdwr-Jones, 1998; Baker *et al.*, 1999; Allmendinger and Tewdwr-Jones, 2000). The requisite synthesis of economic development and planning policies at the regional level requires, the DETR (1999) has argued, 'constructive and collaborative working and on-going dialogue' (para. 22); the various agencies will be drawn together through 'mutual interest' which will entail them working 'constructively together' (para. 23). The Government thus seems to be hoping that a workable set of relations will arise by 'iteration' (see *ibid.* para.22; Chairs of the RDAs, 1999b para. 11).

The DETR (1999b para.22) argues that the strategies of regional agencies 'will need to be complementary if they are to secure the management of change in a coherent and sustainable way'. The emphasis on sustainability runs through all the proposed regional policies, including regional planning:

In drawing up the brief for the RPG review, the RPB and other stakeholders will need to...take account of any relevant objectives, policies and programmes specified in related regional or sub-regional documents. In particular this will include the regional sustainable development framework. The Government made clear in its new UK sustainable development strategy...that such a framework document, as endorsed by the Regional Chamber, should be in place in each region by the end of 2000. These are to be high-level statements of regional vision for achieving sustainable development and will set priorities expressed through regional indicators and targets (*ibid.*).

According to *Guidance on Preparing Regional Sustainable Frameworks* (DETR, 2000c), sustainable development policy in the regions must:

- Define a high-level vision which considers the key social, economic, environmental, and resource issues and the inter-relationship between them.
- Define sustainable development objectives for the region, and set priorities with the help of regional indicators and targets.
- Provide a point of reference for other regional activity showing how all four objectives of the national sustainable development strategy - social, economic, environmental, and resource use - can be met.
- Map out the relationships between the various regional and national initiatives that can contribute to sustainable development in order to minimize duplication.
- Establish a process of monitoring and review taking account of the role envisaged for the framework.

Thus, not only is regional planning policy to be given more autonomy, but it is also to be made more 'sustainable' and should use a range of methods (or 'technologies') in order to achieve this policy goal.

RPG is now to take a strategic approach to regional development in line with its understanding of appropriate levels and distributions of development. As PPG 11 puts it: 'The long-term objective of RPG should be to develop into a comprehensive spatial strategy for the region i.e. to set out the range of public policies that will manage the future distribution of activities within the region' (DETR, 1999b para.4). In short, sustainable regional planning is strategic planning which reflects the needs of regional and sub-regional territories.

It seems apparent then that the Labour administration is concerned to build up the potential of the regional tier. There is a genuine desire to ensure that regional planning does more than simply repeat national policy and that it reflects more readily the variations (economic, social, and environmental) of regional territories. We shall explore the reasons for this in the next chapter. At this juncture it is sufficient to say that if the present proposals achieve their aim, the rationality of 'spatial' or 'sustainable planning' is likely to become much more central to planning policy.

Local policy

Following arguments presented in the last two sections we might be tempted to conclude that planning policy emerges strongly from the central state but that at the present time there is some pressure to 'regionalize' policy, to ensure that a stronger regional tier intervenes between the national state and the local state. Does this mean then that the local state, local government, plays only a minor role in the development of policy?

While it is clear that policy emerges from the central state, it is frequently mentioned, as we have noted, that the UK planning system is a discretionary system (e.g. Cullingworth and Nadin, 1997) and that significant power over the planning policy process remains at the local level. This discretionary power exists because it is assumed that local planning authorities must have some ability to respond to local circumstances. Because local circumstances vary so widely, it is thought inappropriate for central state policy to be too specific or prescriptive. Moreover, planning gains legitimacy through public participation and participation is most easily engineered at the local level (it is often assumed that the public finds strategic thinking difficult to grapple with, although, as we shall see, this assumption is now in need of revision - see also Rydin, 1999). Again, participation is based on the presumption that local planning policy is open to some amendment and must be tailored to local circumstances. It is hard to countenance that so much participation takes place and has no effect (for instance, because policy is strongly shaped by central government). Some amount of discretion, we might argue, must be retained at the local level.

Investigating this issue is made more difficult by the complex structure of local government in the UK. While there are variations in functions across the four countries, the structure of local government in Scotland and Wales is now relatively straightforward (they are governed by unitary authorities at the local level). The situation in England, however, remains complex, with unitary authorities sitting side by side with two-tier authorities, while metropolitan areas have their own structures (currently based on the boroughs and districts). Outside the six metropolitan areas (Greater Manchester, Merseyside, South Yorkshire, Tyne and Wear, West Midlands and West Yorkshire) the planning functions of local government are split between the tiers, with the counties preparing structure plans and the districts preparing local plans (except, of course, in those places that have unitary authorities where only unitary development plans are prepared).

In practice, the counties dominated the development plan system until well into the 1990s, as structure plans provided the only guidance for control in many counties where local plans had not been prepared (district-wide local plans were required under the 1991 Planning and Compensation Act but took a number of years to come into existence). Another major function of the counties has been in the planning and control of minerals and waste disposal and, again, plans for each of these issues are required. The counties also have additional statutory functions in archaeology and coastal protection, with tourism and economic development split between the tiers. The districts were given responsibility for local development plans and most of development control (excluding minerals and wastes).

As we showed in Chapter 2, planning now has an enhanced role at the local level. Thus, Cullingworth and Nadin (1997 p.62) believe that though local government has in many ways been transformed by the shift away from direct service provision to a new role (loosely termed 'strategic enablement' - see Stoker, 2000 for a summary), planning 'as a statutory and regulatory function has been somewhat protected from the pressure for change'. Continuity seems to be the prevailing characteristic of planning at the local level. Although planning offices have often been caught up in broader processes of governmental restructuring, planning policy still remains a discrete part of local government activity and the delivery of that policy is still undertaken in time-honoured fashion.

A sense of continuity can be seen clearly in the implementation of planning policy through development plans. Since the early years of the operation of the planning system, it has been the practice for planning objectives in local areas to be clearly set out in plans so that all interested parties can find guidelines about the likely types and locations of development in a local area. These plans combine strategic and local considerations but for much of the post war period the various functions have, to a certain extent, been divided between different plan types. Thus structure plans provide a strategic policy framework for the whole county, one which seeks to ensure that development in the districts is consistent with national and regional planning policy, while local plans translate the strategic aims into more localized policy and provide detailed guidance on land use.

This division of responsibilities has, on occasion, given rise to some degree of conflict and confusion. Either structure plans have been too directive and detailed, or local plans have diverged from county policy. Moreover, the plans are often formulated at different times and therefore emphasize differing policies. The differential time horizons of plans can lead to further confusion at the local level. The often bewildering nature of the plans has thus led to some ambivalence about their status. They have been seen as both effective and necessary tools in the delivery of planning policy and as symptomatic of excessive regulation in the planning arena. Thus, over the years commentators have stressed both the lack of flexibility, inherent ambiguity and overly detailed nature of local plan policies (e.g. Bruton, 1980) and the role they play in guiding and supporting development control decisions (e.g. Healey *et al.*, 1988).

The shift towards a plan-led system in the early 1990s ostensibly introduced more consistency into the plan-making system. The 1991 Planning and Compensation Act made the local development plan the primary consideration in development control decisions (so as to standardize the status of plans in planning decisions), while also making mandatory the introduction of district-wide plans (the coverage of district-wide plans had previously been quite haphazard with some districts adopting district-wide plans while others just concentrated on areas of development activity). Thus, in the first half of the 1990s, it seemed as though the framework of local planning policy in England was to become more coherent (with PPGs also being used to engineer this coherence).

For much of the post war period development plans have gradually been increasing in scope. Originally they were almost solely concerned with land use issues. However, during the 1960s it became evident that policies around land use could not be adequately formulated unless the broader economic and social trends surrounding development were taken into consideration. Thus, plans became increasingly complex. Although the Conservative governments of the 1980s again began to restrict the scope of plan policies - especially those in structure plans (Thornley, 1993) - local plans still embrace a wide-ranging set of economic and social issues, even though their proposals are still very much focused on land use allocation (Healey, 1983; Bingham, 1997). This increasing complexity undermined uniformity.

Moreover, in the new plan-led system, plan adoption has also become more complex, in part because the increased significance of the plan has been noted by developers, interest groups and local residents leading to their greater involvement in the plan making process (Abram *et al.*, 1996; MacGregor and Ross, 1995). In 1988 an Inspector would have spent an average of seven weeks holding and reporting on a local plan inquiry; by 1995 this figure had increased to fifty weeks, an indication of the larger area covered by plans, higher levels of public participation, and the amount of scrutiny by government agencies (Cullingworth and Nadin, 1997).

Clearly, if plans have an enhanced status then this is likely to provoke great efforts on the part of all concerned interests to influence their policies. And PPG 1, which has amplified the procedures introduced in the 1991 Planning and Compensation Act, states that:

> Because of the role of the development plan in determining the future location of development, it is important that anyone with an interest in the future pattern of development in the plan area should participate in its preparation and help influence its emerging policies (DETR, 1992/1997 para.41).

As Herbert-Young (1995 p.299) says, the plan-led approach 'increases the importance of public participation in the plan-making process' and there is the potential for plan making to become more acrimonious as all parties see it as crucial in determining future development control decisions. Thus it is expected that, greater involvement, together with greater reliance on experts, will almost certainly mean greater delay in plan production, which is contrary to the requirement set out by both the Government and the courts that plans be up to date, specific and relevant (MacGregor and Ross, 1995 p.55).

This heightened participation is especially likely when significant numbers of new houses are to be included in plan policies. At the local level, the impacts of development become easy to see and the figures pose a greater apparent threat than at higher levels of planning. As local activists come to realize that housing development is more easily facilitated if plan policies specify the need for development, so they are more likely to become involved in protracted campaigns during the plan review process (Abram *et al.*, 1996).

Recent attempts to simplify and streamline the planning system in order to make it more efficient and less acrimonious have not been entirely successful, partly for reasons mentioned above. Thus in *Modernizing Planning*, published in 1998, the Labour Government proposes an improvement in plan review processes as a key goal of planning policy. The consultation paper argues that measures should be introduced (in a revised version of PPG 12) that 'promote shorter, clearer plans and better targeted consultation'. However, the Government also claims it is committed to the new partnership activities associated with an 'enabling' local state. Thus, in introducing the consultation paper, John Prescott said:

> Our agenda is the renewal of local democratic government, leading local communities and serving local people. We want councils to gain a new democratic legitimacy....We can achieve this only by working with councils, businesses, professional bodies, the voluntary sector and local people. Equally, within local communities all must work closely together in partnership (DETR, 1998a para 1.8).

Clearly Prescott wishes local government to be as inclusive as possible; it must 'actively promote public participation' in order to 'capture the imagination and enthusiasm of local people' (ibid.). This theme is continued in the White Paper *Modern Local Government: In Touch With the People* also published in 1998: it says 'the Government wishes to see consultation and participation embedded into the culture of all councils... and undertaken across a wide range of each council's responsibilities' (DETR, 1998c para.3.2). These aspirations reinforce the shift to territorial planning. While a number of local participants will be attempting to open development opportunities in the plan, many - if not most - will be seeking to assert environmental and social concerns. Thus, if government aspirations to make development plans genuinely 'collaborative' are met, the thrust of local planning may change markedly: 'development' plans may become 'sustainable development' plans.

Central policy and local discretion

Clearly the aim of increasing local participation is based on the assumption that this participation will be worthwhile; that is, it will allow local actors to influence the policy so that its implementation reflects local aspirations and circumstances (Thomas, 1996). This raises the question of local discretion which is frequently seen as so central to the UK planning system. As Cullingworth and Nadin (1997 p.82) say:

> the approach adopted in Britain, which is in many important ways the same in the 1990s as it was in the 1950s, is fundamentally a discretionary one in which decisions on particular development proposals are made as they arise against the policy background of a generalized plan.

However, as we saw in Chapter 2, the relationship between local discretion and generalized policy is in a state of constant flux and this has led some to argue that new policy frameworks - such as the PPGs and the plan-led approach - have eroded the degree of local discretion that exists in both local plans and development control decision making (Allmendinger and Tewdwr-Jones, 1997). We must therefore briefly assess the balance between the two sides of planning policy.

As mentioned previously, the emergence of the PPG system coincided with the shift towards a plan-led system. PPGs have made themselves felt at the local level through their inclusion in development plans. As development plans emerge they necessarily include planning policy as prescribed by the guidance notes. In fact, PPG 1 (DETR, 1997 para.44) says that since the commencement of a plan-led approach

> the Secretary of State has been examining development plans carefully to identify whether they are consistent with national and regional planning guidance and whether there are conflicts with the guidance which do not appear to be justified by local circumstances.

A key issue becomes, then, the extent to which the plan-led approach, and with it the top-down nature of planning policy guidance, have curtailed the amount of local discretion. There has been much debate about this in the literature with some commentators arguing that the plan-led approach has ushered in a fundamentally changed system, where the balance between local discretion and national policy has swung markedly in favour of the latter, while others have argued that in practice the new approach has made very little difference (see Cullingworth and Nadin, 1997; Vigar *et al.*, 2000).

To a considerable degree this debate hinges on the interpretation given to Section 54A of the 1991 Planning and Compensation Act which, it is worth repeating, states: 'Where, in making any determination under the planning Acts, regard is to be had to the development plan, the determination shall be made in accordance with the plan unless material considerations indicate otherwise'. It was the insertion of this paragraph into the Bill that is deemed to have ushered in the plan-led approach. Section 54A effectively emerged during the debate over the Bill in the House of Commons. The then opposition (Labour) spokesperson on planning, Clive Soley, proposed an amendment to the Bill so that development plans would have higher status. By this point the government had also come to perceive the need for a strengthening of the plan's role, with Sir George Young, the then Minister for Housing and Planning, stating that the government wished to strengthen the role of the development plan in 'every' planning decision and that it wanted to 'make clear to local planning authorities and others how to go about making the decision'. A consensus therefore quickly emerged between the two parties around the need for Section 54A (see the discussion in Herbert-Young, 1995).

It would seem that the Conservative government's (and the Labour opposition's) intention was to strengthen the role of the development plan to make it more central to local decision making. A great deal of legal argument has thus ensued which tries to clarify the extent to which the plan is now the key determinant of local development control. Michael Purdue (1994), for instance, believes that development plan policies will cover almost all development control decisions. A key issue becomes, then, the balance in decision making between the development plan and 'material considerations'. While it is generally accepted that there is a presumption in favour of the plan, 'appropriate' weight still needs to be given to other issues (Purdue, 1994 p.402), although there is scope for debate about the meaning of the word 'appropriate'. It seems that the incorporation of material considerations cannot dictate that a decision be made other than in accordance with the plan but such considerations can be used to indicate the need for some flexibility in reaching decisions that do not fully accord with plan policies. Often this local flexibility can be interpreted in the following terms:

> The extent to which a development accords with the purposes, or substance, of development plan policies, rather than the exact terms of every relevant policy, appears to be a fundamental consideration in the application of Section 54A... (Herbert-Young, 1995 p.301).

Furthermore, it is abundantly clear that development plan policies are often open to multiple interpretations, and that different policies also pull in different directions. This again highlights some scope for local discretion in interpretation and application.

In fact, all the protagonists in debates around these issues recognize that some flexibility is essential to the system (e.g. Herbert-Young, 1995 p.297), but one group of authors believe that Section 54A has made a significant difference to the role of the development plan, especially compared to the situation which prevailed in the mid-1980s when the government seemed to be systematically downgrading the status of plans in favour of other considerations. They believe

Section 54A has led to 'a greater emphasis upon the development plan in development control' (Herbert-Young, 1995 p.305). A more sceptical approach to section 54A is taken in a couple of articles by Ian Gatenby and Christopher Williams (1992; 1996). These authors effectively argue that the clause makes little difference to local decision making and say,

> there will almost always ·be material considerations apart from the development plan, and in our opinion the weight to be given to them will be a matter for the judgement of the decision maker who will be entitled to decide that they override the development plan (1992 p.120).

While Gatenby and Williams accept that the government has introduced a plan-led approach, they believe that in practice it has not unduly affected the amount of local discretion. Likewise, Michael Bingham (1997 p.35) in a study of the coverage of local plans in the plan-led system accepts that coverage has been extended and policies have become more detailed but he doubts that plans are becoming more 'prescriptive'. So again, support for the notion of 'local discretion' can be found.

It would appear therefore that, though planning policy has moved in favour of stronger national guidance within the context of a greater role for the local development plan, there is still scope for local discretion in the interpretation and application of policies. What most commentators seem to agree upon, however, is that Section 54A has altered people's perceptions of the plan formulation process. Whether or not local decisions are always made in accordance with the plan, there is a widespread recognition, promoted by government, that plan reviews are a key point of influence, so all those interested in planning decisions must get involved in the review process. Thus, the plan-led approach has encouraged greater participation and seems to imply that local people will use the discretion that exists to tailor policies to their own requirements in line with local (developmental and environmental) circumstances.

This raises a key question: to what extent can participants in the review processes actually influence the interpretation and incorporation of policy in local plans? Clearly, the involvement of so many people for such sustained periods of time must be seen as some kind of testament to their ability to influence outcomes in plan review processes. However, research on this issue tends to find a great deal of disappointment amongst many participants who believe that their involvement has not really changed anything to any great extent (Abram *et al.*, 1996; Vigar *et al.*, 2000). Some studies indicate that the major decisions have been taken prior to the review process (Hull and Vigar, 1995; Murdoch *et al.*, 1999; see also Chapter 5 below), while others complain that national policy is so strong little can be achieved locally except the implementation of such policy almost unchanged (Allmendinger and Tewdwr-Jones, 1997; Vigar *et al.*, 2000). One issue that all commentators tend to agree upon, however, is that the balance between national prescription and local discretion varies according to sector and according to geographical location. In some sectors the amount of discretion available at the local level is high, while in others it is low. In some geographical areas planning authorities adhere rigidly to central policy, in others they engage in considerable local interpretation. We explore these issues further in the next chapter where we describe the formulation of national policy in the planning for housing sector to investigate the amount of local discretion permitted within that particular policy sector. In the following two chapters we situate the analysis very firmly within one geographical location - Buckinghamshire in the south east of England - in order to consider how national policies coalesce with the territorial aspirations of local participants.

Conclusion

The planning policy framework is complex, with responsibilities distributed amongst a number of agencies operating at the different tiers of government. It is therefore often difficult to determine which agency or tier is responsible for policy, thereby making it hard to give a definitive answer to the question - 'where does planning policy come from?' However, we can see that the central state plays a key role in developing national policy, notably through the PPGs, and that this policy serves to provide some consistency and uniformity across the system. Whether one takes the view that PPGs determine the content of local development plans or argues that they simply provide loose guidelines very much in line with local discretion, it is clear that they are an effective way of quickly and directly disseminating central state thinking to regional and local authorities. They illustrate that, in planning policy, rationalities of planning are closely tied to the technologies of implementation.

In the context of the plan-led system, PPGs serve to shape local development outcomes. The plan-led approach also specifies that local plans must be developed collectively by a range of local stakeholders ('local plans for local people', so to speak). It would therefore appear that development plans combine national and local discourses, but that the balance between the two must be investigated in any given instance (both in terms of geographical area and the policy sector). However, given our general thesis here that planning is gradually adopting a new 'territorial' rationality, it seems likely that the balance between these two aspects is swinging towards the local.

Yet there is little evidence for this at the local level itself. Commentators still complain that, in practice, local views are sidelined by national policy (see, for instance, Vigar *et al.*, 2000). More compelling evidence that the balance is changing is currently emerging at the regional tier. Here, government is seeking to introduce a form of regional planning that is more clearly embedded in regional territories - for instance, it wishes to encourage regional 'ownership' of RPG so that policies reflect more closely the views and aspirations of regional stakeholders. It is our view that this approach, especially when it is allied to the goal of 'regional sustainable development', will encourage the shift away from uniform national policy towards a much more regionalized form of planning. As a consequence policy in some regions will subscribe to the rationality of 'planning for development' (notably the north east where economic growth is seen as much more necessary than environmental protection), while other regions will subscribe to the rationality of 'planning for sustainable development' (notably the south east where economic growth is plentiful).

Moreover, this enhanced status for regional planning implies a reconfiguration in the planning policy hierarchy in ways that might make it difficult for national policy to flow easily down to the local level: this policy may now get 'bogged down' in the spatialized approaches of the regions. Local planning authorities may then find themselves confronted with conflicting advice as PPGs and RPGs diverge. In these circumstances it will be interesting to see how national government responds: will it be happy to let 'regional flowers' bloom or will it seek to re-impose an abstract and decontextualized national policy? We return to this question in Chapter 7.

Chapter 4

Planning by Numbers

Introduction

Previous chapters have shown that the amount of local discretion in the planning system varies over time according to the changing relationships between national and local policy and, as we mentioned, between sectors, with some sectors yielding more freedom for local action than others. The PPG system coalesces with the plan-led approach to ensure some degree of uniformity in planning policy across various local authority areas. However, while the PPGs specify plan content they are vague enough to allow some degree of variation in interpretation. Other modes of central regulation also give flexibility at the local level.

For instance, Patsy Healey (1999) has argued that, in contrast to many other areas of planning, national planning policy has had little to say about the allocation of land for employment purposes. Traditionally, policy has exhorted local planning authorities not to obstruct economic development unless absolutely necessary and has asked them to keep a range of sites available to meet different types of demand for land. Some increased national regulation has accompanied the emergence of the sustainability agenda since the early 1990s, particularly as regards the need to locate employment premises in ways that reduce travel. Overall, however, Healey says 'there was little coherence in the expression of national planning policy in relation to site allocation for economic development purposes' (1999 p.31). Local planning authorities have therefore largely been given scope to determine their own strategies towards economic development. Healey concludes that, in the case of land for industrial development local authorities frequently 'write their own script' (*ibid.*).

Other sectors display different sets of central-local relations. For instance, it has long been recognized that formalized central direction is particularly significant in two sectors: minerals and housing. Angela Hull (1997 p.368) writes that,

> What has emerged in the 1980s is a highly structured process for planning for housing growth and similarly for mineral extraction, where local level decisions on land allocation and development permits are tied into national level projections of demand. These are the only two policy sectors within the British land use planning system which explicitly incorporate a tiered spatial approach - from national to regional to local levels....

In these two sectors there is apparently little scope for any of the tiers to go their own way (for a comparison of the two sectors - see Cowell and Murdoch, 1999). Thus, regional and local planning arenas find themselves tied into a fairly prescriptive set of governmental relationships. In this chapter we focus on housing and examine the extent to which the central state is giving formal direction through the 'hierarchical arrangements' that characterize planning in this sector (planning for housing is also the focus of the case studies presented in chapters 5 and 6).

In our view, housing is a particularly apt arena in which to study both the changing structure of governance and the emergence of new planning rationalities. Planning for housing has traditionally been dominated by the concern to promote housing development (in line with demand) and the whole mode of government in the sector has been ordered according to this rationale. Yet, as previous chapters have shown, planning in this sector is now extremely controversial, with a number of trends - environmentalism, counterurbanization, public participation in a plan-led system - converging so that a great deal of pressure has been placed on this policy area. This pressure is aimed at replacing the rationality of development with a rationality of spatial complexity.

The sector also provides a useful case study because the dominant rationality has clearly been underpinned by governmental technologies. We pay particular attention to these technologies, notably the use of projections to link the various tiers of government together. In understanding the role of the projections, we wish to clarify whether they open up a 'conduit of power' (Rose, 1991) from centre to locale, or whether they are more tenuous in nature, leaving scope for local interpretation. In short, we consider whether the projections are based on 'discipline' or 'discretion'. We thus examine the traditional usage of the figures in the planning system and show how the numbers cascade down the planning hierarchy. We then discuss recent changes to the system and ask whether these changes will 'embed' the numerical governmentalities in spatial complexity, thereby loosening their hold on the entire planning for housing system.

Planning for future housing demand

According to Vigar *et al.* (2000, especially Chapter 4), the allocation of land for housing has been a long-standing policy commitment in English planning. However, 'throughout the 1980s and 1990s, this particular policy task was given a high priority: to identify appropriate locations for new housing and ensure that sufficient land was available to meet society's housing needs' (Vigar *et al.*, 2000 p.91). These authors show that planning for housing has traditionally been a 'technical' activity in which sites were identified using local population projections as a surrogate for likely future demand. Local housing allocation policies were managed by the development plan process, although the powers of the plan 'waxed' and 'waned' in line with central government policy (see Chapter 2 above). During the 1980s, however, a more formal system of predicting demand - and therefore the amount of housing land required - was consolidated at the national level. Central government engaged in forecasting future levels of demand and passed these forecasts down through the planning hierarchy to the local level. These forecasts acted to define a formal set of relations between the various tiers of government - central, regional, county and district - and were used to ensure that local authority designations meshed with national requirements, so that the various agencies at all spatial scales worked to meet future housing demand.

In planning to meet future demand, a key issue became the extent to which planning authorities could predict future housing growth with any degree of accuracy. In other words, how could these authorities ensure that decisions taken in the present really did meet the needs of future generations? And could they perform this task in ways that are segregated from the pro- and anti-development politics that, as we saw in chapters 1 and 2, are so ubiquitous in the planning arena?

Clearly, in undertaking the forecasting activity, techniques were required that allowed an educated guess to be made about future housing demands and requirements. And these techniques should be somehow detached from the 'push and pull' of ordinary politics; ideally, they should have legitimacy amongst all those seeking to influence planning outcomes. The most appropriate technology for these purposes was the forecasts of housing demand. These forecasts asserted that future demands are calculable in terms which bear some correspondence to likely outcomes. The forecasts were calculated, in the main, on the basis of past trends extrapolated into the future. Trend planning thus lay at the heart of the planning for housing system (Allinson, 1999). It is thus worth briefly outlining how the forecasts are constructed.

In developing the projections of future housing demand, planning departments assess household formation trends using information derived from the decennial census. The census is the most comprehensive source of statistical data in the UK; it provides complete coverage of contemporary demographic and social changes and allows for detailed examination of such changes at the local level (Jackson, 1998). The census is complemented by the mid-year estimates of population change. These estimates are based on figures from the previous census with allowance for births, deaths, migration and ageing and they form the basis for population projections, which are made every two years. Essentially, the projections provide an estimate of the future population of the UK, one calculated on assumptions derived from current demographic statistics. The DETR produces detailed household projections every three years or so, based upon the most recent population projections. The household projections adopt the same definition of a household as the census, namely 'one person living alone, or a group of people who share common housekeeping or a living room'. The approach used is to 'classify people into groups based on some close relationship or affinity i.e. by family ties, marriage, cohabitation or close friendship, so that each group can be seen to represent a requirement for a separate dwelling' (DoE, 1995 p.46). According to the DoE (1995 p.12), the household projections are compiled by applying projected household membership rates to the projections of the private household population disaggregated by age, gender and marital/cohabitational status, and summing the resulting projections of household representatives.

The institutional population - those in prison, residential care, etc. - is then subtracted from the total to give a level of demand for housing. For the household projections, rates of household formation within each age, gender and marital status grouping are extrapolated into the future on the basis of observed rates from the last census (using the so-called 'life-cycle method' which presumes that the household membership rates in a given cohort will vary smoothly over time).

The implications of the projections are then assessed in terms of the demand for housing. A four-stage approach is used, which begins with the forecasts of household growth and estimates of how much the total demand will be met through owner-occupation. This is again done by extrapolating forward current trends in home ownership. Assumptions are also made about the amount of housing demand that will be met through the private rented sector and, once the owner occupation figure is added to this, an assumption is made about the amount of social housing that will be required. As the DoE has stressed (1995 p.14), the whole methodology is largely based 'on rolling forward current patterns of behaviour and existing trends'. It does not attempt to model either policy change or economic change and therefore 'inevitably incorporates a large degree of uncertainty' (DoE, 1995 p.15). The projections cannot then 'be regarded as precise predictions of future years and the sources of uncertainty have to be borne in mind'. Furthermore, 'uncertainty increases with the degree of detail, both geographically and by category of household, and with distance into the future' (DoE, 1995 p.13).

The purpose of the projections is to aid forward planning and to ensure that planning meets the Government's objective of a 'decent home within reach of every family' (with a subsidiary aim that of allowing migratory trends to be - as far as possible - freely expressed so that an 'efficient' labour market can be promoted - see House of Commons, 1998 para.44). The role of planning is therefore to 'provide an adequate and continuous supply of housing' (according to PPG 3 *Housing* – DETR 2000b). In order for planning to fulfil this role all tiers of the planning hierarchy need to work towards the same overall numbers. Thus, once a set of national projections has been derived, they are translated into regional and local housing requirements. In effect, the projections tie together the various tiers of government.

According to projections published in 1995, the number of households in England looked set to grow from 19.2 million in 1991 to 23.6 million in 2016, an increase of 23 per cent. The reasons for this increase were summarized by DoE (1995 p.13) as:

- A projected growth in the total adult private household population.
- Change in the age structure of the population (people are getting older).
- Changes in marital status (number of divorces and amount of co-habitation).
- Changes in the rates at which different households form.

These factors were also underpinned by a further set of assumptions concerning such issues as external and internal migration. While the previous set of projections had assumed nil net international migration, in the 1995 projections the international migration figures assumed that 50,000 more people would enter England than would leave during the forecast period (this assumption became a source of some criticism - see for instance, Bate, 1999). The projections stipulated that 4.4 million new homes would be needed by 2016. Just under half (46 per cent) this total was attributed to the increase in population, half a million of which was estimated to come from in-migration. The most significant increase, however, came from the projected changes in the rate of household formation due to late marriage, separation, divorce and co-habitation (33 per cent of the total). More recent (1999) projections suggested that a slightly lower number of households would form up to 2016 (3.8 million).

The '4.4 million' figure launched planning for housing policy into a fierce debate between developers, government agencies, environmental groups, and rural residents about the appropriate scale and distribution of new housing. This debate, which rumbled on throughout the latter half of the 1990s, led to calls for a downgrading of the projections and the assertion of alternative modes of calculation so that the spatial contexts of new housing could be given greater prominence. In short, a debate took place between two rationalities of planning: planning for housing development (via the numbers) and planning for sustainable development (via a stronger spatial contextualization of the numbers).

Descending the hierarchy

The first stop on the way down the planning hierarchy for the projections is regional planning guidance. Although we argued in the previous chapter that regional planning is the weakest tier of planning in England, it has played a role in planning for new housing (a role that, as we shall see, is growing stronger at the current time). As the projections of future demand are 'parcelled out' to the regions so they are to be assessed against other regional factors (rather than being simply passed unchanged down the hierarchy to the counties and districts). According to DoE (1996), in any review of RPG the factors to be taken into account when reaching the recommendation for new housing are:

- Current number of households in the region.
- Surveys of current housing, by dwelling type.
- Estimates of housing vacancy rates.
- Appraisals of regional dynamics (e.g. state of the economy).
- Estimates of tied accommodation and second homes.
- Estimates of need for replacement dwelling and refurbishment.
- Scope for conversions and changes in use for offices, etc.

Once all these estimates and sources of data have been considered then a regional figure can be calculated for the RPG period. In theory, the regional housing figures should be a mix of national housing requirements and specific regional conditions (such as state of the regional environment and its capacity to accommodate new houses). However, while the regional housing figures have undoubtedly been determined through agreement between county council representatives, central government civil servants and others such as the HBF and the CPRE, there is some evidence that a certain amount of 'arm twisting' has been used, with central government acting as the final arbiter in any dispute (see House of Commons, 1998 para.32). As Vigar *et al.* (2000 p.94) put it, 'increasingly during the 1990s, the national government was prepared to intervene to ensure that the administrative tiers of government accept the hierarchical cascade of housing growth responsibilities'.

Once a regional figure for the required houses has been agreed then it is divided between the various unitary and county authorities that make up the regional planning authority. Taking the regional figure as a starting point, the counties employ similar processes to those existing at the regional level in distributing the total amongst the districts to be included in local plans. They attempt to 'ground' the figures in a range of contextual circumstances in order to decide both scale and distribution of housing development during the plan period. The main difference is the amount of public consultation around the plans at these lower levels of the hierarchy. During the course of structure and local plan reviews it is supposed that the figures can be 'tested' (DoE, 1996) as all interested parties debate the projections and their likely local impacts. The debates, in theory at least, can lead to an amendment of the county or district totals. However, Wenban-Smith (1998 para.12), commenting on the past operation of the policy hierarchy, says:

> On the face of it this is an open process with several opportunities to articulate local and regional views. In practice the system is operated in centralist fashion. In particular, the [DETR] has sought to impose regional housing provisions corresponding to their regional allocation of the national household projection and has usually succeeded.

Vigar *et al.* (2000 pp.91-93) likewise argue that 'by the 1990s, allocating land for housing had become a relatively closed, hierarchical policy area'. They point out that this was largely because local residents had come to perceive new housing sites 'as a threat to their quality of life'. With the introduction of the plan-led system in the early 1990s, and the encouragement this gave to local participation, national government was faced with the problem of finding sufficient land for new housing *through* the local plan process. The solution to this problem was an enhanced use of the housing projections.

To summarize, we can see that abstract categories and forms of calculation lie at the heart of the planning for housing system. Statistical techniques, surveys, estimates and so on, drive the planning system into ensuring that housing will be provided for future generations. The abstractions and calculations are piled up in the forecasting system; they relate not just to current trends and structures but to the way these are thought to be extended into the future. Because the projections are complex, and because they contain so many assumptions and estimates, they come laden with 'health warnings'. The DoE (1996 p.4) says: 'as with any set of estimates covering such a long time period, the household projections cannot be regarded as precise predictions of all future years'. And the DoE (1995) believes that this lack of precision is magnified as the projections descend down to particular geographical contexts (see also Bramley, 1998; Bramley and Watkins, 1996). Yet in practice, as the projections make this descent, they become difficult to resist, and therefore often greatly determine the numbers of houses built in local areas (see chapters 5 and 6 below).

In part, this contradiction can be explained by the overall reliance of planners in this sector on the figures. Without the projections it would be almost impossible to guess how many houses would be needed over given time horizons and therefore land shortages would undoubtedly occur. Thus, the discourse of uncertainty which surrounds the figures is frequently held in check, despite the criticisms levelled at their use (e.g. there is a circularity at the local level, they take no account of economic factors, many of the underlying assumptions are unreliable and so on - see Bate, 1999). The following comment is fairly typical: 'Although there are uncertainties attached to the figures, the latest household projections are the best assessment that can be made with currently available information and the broad picture of significant household growth is not in doubt' (John Prescott in House of Commons, 1998 para.1154). In fact, almost all those agencies that have investigated the use of the figures in planning for housing tend to endorse this view. Two House of Commons Environment Select Committees have concluded that the figures are 'valid' and are the best estimates of new households currently available (see House of Commons, 1995; 1998; DETR, 1998b; this view is also supported by the Joseph Rowntree Foundation, the TCPA and the RTPI - see Breheny and Hall, 1996). Moreover, more critical commentators (such as Glen Bramley, who has produced work for the CPRE show that the projections have a circular character at the local level - that is, as more households are predicted so more homes are built so more households form or move into the area and take up the homes, etc.), believe that 'they are clearly the best projections because they are the only ones we have and it is quite difficult to produce a different set of projections using a different system. There is no alternative system that is so well developed' (Bramley, 1998 para. 21).

The main significance of the figures for the analysis being outlined here is that they codify the relationships between the various governmental agencies involved in planning and appear to facilitate central direction of the whole system. The central state is responsible for undertaking calculations of future housing demand and for ensuring that these are passed down the hierarchy. The regional state must adopt a figure which accords with the national total and then must distribute this out to the counties. The counties must ensure that the figure accords with their requirements and available land resources. The districts must ensure that land is available to meet its housing allocations under the structure plan. And all these distributions and allocations must be conducted in line with PPG policy (in this case, PPG 3). The relations between all the tiers are therefore strongly prescribed and the prescriptions are, in the main, carried by numerical technologies of government. For this reason we can say that the numbers are a 'disciplinary', rather than 'discretionary', technology.

The spatialization of planning for housing policy

As the figures descend the hierarchy so they become more tangible; that is, as they get closer to ground level, the developmental consequences of the projections become clearer as district councils must find sites to meet their housing quotas. The translation of the figures down the hierarchy brings the local impacts slowly into view so that eventually the numbers are translated into sites and then houses in the local landscape (as we shall see in chapters 5 and 6, it is here that the numbers get embedded in many complex local considerations). Concern about the impacts of the figures has thus come to focus on the way levels of local housing development seem to be 'driven' by the projections. The CPRE (1995 p.132), for instance, argues that the 'household projections have a profound effect on decisions made about new housing development'. In the view of this environmental NGO, the figures determine local level decision making around new housing development; they are 'the fundamental driver of the planning for housing process' (*ibid.* p.132). In other words, the demands of future generations for housing are imposed on local decision makers so as to ensure that all these future households have access to a decent home. The CPRE view is that the figures have a 'coercive' character; local participants in plan reviews have to accept the figures and it is impossible for them to come up with viable alternatives. In short, the figures act to delimit debate at the local level (Murdoch and Abram, 1998).

These concerns were brought to a head with the publication of the 4.4 million forecast. Following the furore about this projection, John Major's government opened up what it called a 'great housing debate'. Faced with the prospect, in the run up to a general election, of developing a policy which would allocate land for an extra 4.4 million new homes (half of which were to be located in the south of England), the Conservatives attempted to delay any planning policy decisions. Upon coming to power, Labour's Environment Secretary, John Prescott, inherited this debate and quickly found it to be one of the most intractable confronting the new government.

The problems facing the new Labour government in dealing with the housing issue stemmed from a perception that it is primarily an urban party, with little understanding of rural sensibilities. Thus, a suspicion quickly emerged (in part, because it was promoted by groups such as the Countryside Alliance) that Labour would countenance extensive house building in the countryside. In response, John Prescott made a number of policy pronouncements aimed at countering this view. In the process, the contours of a new policy gradually began to emerge (although it should be noted that we use the term 'new' cautiously here given that a number of commentators believe Labour's proposals were originally envisaged by the Major government - see Allmendinger and Tewdwr-Jones, 2000).

To begin with, Prescott made a great virtue out of rejecting what he called the 'predict and provide' approach - that is predicting the number of new houses needed and simply imposing this figure on regional and local plans. He was now opting, he said, for a more 'responsive' and 'flexible' method of allocating land for housing. He claimed that 'no one can with any certainty predict how many extra households will exist in twenty years time' (DETR, 1998b). The Government should therefore desist from making long terms plans: it should simply set an annual target and ensure that planning authorities 'monitor' and 'manage' the release of land so that this release can be amended in line with ever shifting levels of demand. By 'monitoring and managing', it was claimed planning could better assess the demand for housing at any given moment and the capacity of regional and local areas to accommodate it.

The concern with 'capacity' led on to a commitment to promote 'sustainable patterns of development'. This meant that most new housing (at least 60%) should be concentrated in existing conurbations. In order to achieve 'sustainable development' patterns, planning authorities would be expected to use 'urban capacity studies' to show how urban areas might accommodate more growth and a 'sequential test' which stipulates that brownfield land is utilized before greenfield land (these initiatives were eventually codified in a revised version of PPG 3 published in 2000 - DETR, 2000b). Through the deployment of these two planning tools, local planning authorities will be able to avoid 'inefficient' (i.e. low density) uses of land.

Because central government had come to be blamed for imposing housing figures on local authorities, the DETR was also looking to enhance the responsibility of the regions for the figures. Following the row around the projections, the government published *Planning for the Communities of the Future* in 1998. This document emphasized the need to move away from a top-down structure of planning for housing. John Prescott argued that he wanted to 'decentralize decision making and bring it closer to the people where it counts' (DETR, 1998b). However, he also recognized that some degree of strategic decision making was required to ensure that local authorities do not just refuse development in order to placate local protectionists. Thus the document says that the Government is proposing to increase the responsibility of Regional Planning Conferences (RPCs) in deciding how to best meet housing needs in each region. The RPC is given a key role in adjudicating over conflicts around housing development. *Planning for the Communities of the Future* says that:

> the RPC would discuss with the GOR and development and conservation interests within the region how the region could best accommodate the projected figures. This process of negotiation will improve the local ownership of the numbers; it is also likely to generate a number of options which may include not meeting the projections in full (DETR, 1998b para.6).

Following the RPC report it will then be up to the Secretary of State to decide whether the recommended figures are acceptable. Once the RPG is published, the presumption would be that the housing figures will be reflected in structure plans and UDPs.

This policy shift was codified in PPG 11 on regional planning (DETR, 1999b), which was published in draft form early in 1999. It states that the new PPG,

> places greater responsibility on regional planning bodies, working with the Government Offices and regional stakeholders, to resolve planning issues at the regional level through the production of draft RPG. This will promote greater local ownership of regional policies and increased commitment to their implementation through the statutory planning process (DETR, 1999b p.3).

Thus, responsibility for reviewing regional planning policy is given to the regions themselves. Once the regional planning authorities have produced draft regional guidance then it will be subject to a public examination (overseen by an independent panel) before being issued by the Secretary of State. PPG 11 emphasizes that a 'collective view' must be taken of regional objectives, with a whole variety of stakeholders involved in the formulation of this view (it specifies that the stakeholders should include development agencies, environmental bodies, business organizations, transport providers, utility companies, developers, voluntary groups and women's organisations) (DETR, 1999b p.10).

The new policy contextualizes the projections at the regional level and appears to raise the profile of regional space. It seeks to ensure that a regional 'ownership' of the figures is developed so that the system can be characterized as responsive to regional demands and sensibilities. Regional planning authorities are to take more responsibility for deciding how housing numbers are to be met. In so doing, they must give considerable weight to the spatial implications of development. For instance, it is emphasized that the impact of development on greenfield land must be minimized, therefore regional planning fora must look closely at the allocation of previously developed sites, the scope for a 'sequential' and 'phased' approach, and should have greater awareness of regional development capabilities. Of equal importance is the suggestion that regional planning fora undertake 'sustainability appraisals' which 'should appraise the potential impacts of different strategic options in order to integrate sustainable development objectives in the formulation of policies' (DETR 1999b p.15).

We can see, then, that the housing projections will no longer move through the regions untouched by local contextual factors: they are to be plunged into spatial complexity. This point was emphasized by a DETR civil servant in evidence to the House of Commons Environment Select Committee when he argued that the aim of the new policy is

> to move to a system in which local authorities are given more responsibility for drawing up regional strategies that address not just housing, but transport, economic, social and other issues in the round, and these strategies need to set the long term direction. They will take account of the household projections clearly, but these would only just be one factor. They would be subject to a proper environmental or sustainability appraisal and what actually happens on the ground would then be monitored (House of Commons, 1998 para.211).

The negotiations at the regional level are now to be critical in determining how many houses are actually built, for it appears that the regional planning authorities are being given scope to challenge the figures coming down from above. Thus, under the new arrangements the national figures may not even get as far as the regional plans before they are amended or displaced. The regions, along with the counties and districts, may develop approaches that diverge markedly from those prescribed at the national level. The consequence is that the projections may fail to tie the planning for housing hierarchy together. Thus, we might follow Vigar *et al.* (2000 p.117) in concluding that,

> the "housing numbers game" [shows] signs of having played out its utility. With more stakeholders getting involved, it will be harder to keep political choices within the framework of technical calculation. With more local power to frame policy agendas, it will be difficult to isolate the location of housing from other dimensions of place quality.

Planning for housing in the south east

We can illustrate how the emerging regional capacities are leading to a much stronger spatial contextualization of the figures by briefly examining planning for housing in the south east. The discussion in this section serves two purposes. Firstly, it gives further credence to the argument being proposed here that the 'regionalization' of planning for housing policy will 'slow' the descent of the housing projections. Secondly, the debates examined in this section provide some insight into the types of concerns that are foremost in the south east, the regional context for our study area in chapters 5 and 6 (Buckinghamshire).

Regional planning, as we argued above, has long had the role of situating housing projections in contextual regional circumstances but has been constrained in its ability to fully undertake this task by central government's insistence that the regional figures demarcated in the national housing projections are met in every instance. The Labour government's amendments to the system seem, however, to open up scope for the regions to 'go their own way'. Regional 'ownership' of regional plans appears to promise diminished central government intervention. Nowhere has this policy shift been more welcome than in the south east. Here, levels of housing demand have traditionally been high, but - as we saw earlier, in Chapter 2 - the desire for environmental protection is also strong, particularly in the rural areas of the shire counties. Local planning authorities thus find themselves caught between national obligations and unpopular local policies. In order to escape this uncomfortable situation they have looked to the regional planning forum - SERPLAN - to diminish their national obligations, notably in the form of lower housing numbers.

SERPLAN began to explore the scope for amending the housing figures within Labour's new policy during the latest review of regional planning guidance. Right at the very start of the review, the regional planning authority situated development in the context of regional capabilities. It did this by conducting what it called a 'regional capability study' (SERPLAN, 1997). This study was designed, firstly, to give a comprehensive overview of the region's environment and land resource and, secondly, to demonstrate the key impacts and consequences associated with accommodating alternative theoretical levels and distributions of housing growth (SERPLAN, 1997 p.1). SERPLAN was here attempting to assess the land-use consequences of adopting various levels of new housing development. In short, it was undertaking the sustainability study that the DETR now says should be central to regional policy (see Chapter 3 above).

When the capability study was published it showed that the region could accommodate no more than 914,000 houses if environmental constraints were to remain intact. Thus, the capability study effectively allowed SERPLAN to challenge the national housing projections which indicated that 1.1 million new households would form in the region between 1996 and 2016. In fact the authority proposed that the region should only accommodate around 800,000 new dwellings during the plan period. The rationale used to support this lower figure was based on two assumptions: firstly, the trend to independent living would slow down; secondly, many single people would fail to secure the economic means to enter the housing market. On this basis, SERPLAN argued that it only needed to plan for 75-80 per cent of the new single person households (see SERPLAN, 1998).

In its regional planning guidance preparations, SERPLAN thus attempted to bring the housing figures 'down to earth': the projections were set within a vast range of complicating factors (couched in the language of 'sustainable development' - SERPLAN's draft regional strategy was in fact called *A Sustainable Development Strategy for the South East*). The main strategic approach was based on a belief that past patterns of development in the region were 'unsustainable' (e.g. development gives rise to population dispersal, urban sprawl, and car-based travel) and it was argued that an adequate response to such patterns was the 'central issue' for the regional strategy. Sustainability criteria (e.g. protection of critical regional assets and efficient management of environmental resources) thus shaped the various policies. So, importantly, scale and distribution of development were to be firmly embedded in the context of a regional environment that has various environmental goods in need of protection.

It was evident that SERPLAN was beginning to take up the opportunities offered by John Prescott in *Planning for the Communities of the Future* and PPG 11. In short, the region was attempting to extricate itself from a planning-for-housing system strongly configured by housing projections. The draft regional strategy justified this move by pushing the discourse of sustainable development towards the centre of regional planning policy (SERPLAN was also displacing the housing numbers using another technology of government - the capability study.)

SERPLAN's assertion of a much more spatialized system of planning for housing was then scrutinized by a government appointed Panel in the context of an examination-in-public. The EiP collated the various representations that had been made on the draft regional planning guidance (around 800 in all) and invited selected representatives to debate the RPG policies (in fact, those invited were the 'usual suspects' - developers, environmental and amenity organizations, government agencies and a few local groups such as parish councils). The EiP Panel's report was published in the autumn of 1999 and it provided a critical assessment of SERPLAN's attempt to shift the balance of policy considerations towards sustainable development (Report of Panel, 1999).

In particular, the Panel proclaimed it was not convinced by SERPLAN's spatial strategy as it felt the approach was not capable of meeting regional demands for housing and jobs. The Panel argued that 'the essence of planning lies in taking a view of what is likely to happen in the future and planning to meet it' (1999 p.47) and it urged SERPLAN to 'adopt a reasonable and responsible approach to future housing requirements, taking due account of the household projections' (1999 p.48). In short, the Panel rejected SERPLAN's view that the projections were flawed or that the required level of housing would 'unacceptably compromise other objectives', notably those associated with 'sustainable development' (*ibid.*). It argued that there were no regional factors that were so pressing or so urgent that the figures should be undermined or changed (the figures were therefore given priority over the capability study.)

Unsurprisingly, the reaction to the Panel's report corresponded to the two competing discourses that have been mentioned in this and earlier chapters. For instance, the CPRE (1999 p.2) argued that the report 'flatly contradicts the many recent improvements which the Government has made to land use planning...'. Again, the CPRE argued that RPG must 'recognize the limited environmental capacity of the region as a whole in terms of demands on natural resources' (*ibid.*). Such a recognition would entail a reduction in housing targets. Likewise, SERPLAN (1999 p.3) argued that it had taken up the Government's proposal that household projections are just one of a range of factors that need to be considered so that 'there is a better chance that housing provision can be made in ways which embrace the wider Government and SERPLAN objectives on sustainable development'. SERPLAN also expressed concern about the 'out-of-date attitude' adopted by the Panel towards the concept of sustainable development. However, other commentators came out in support of the Panel report, with the Director of the Town and Country Planning Association, Graeme Bell, calling it a 'masterpiece' (see *Planning* 15th October 1999).

After considering the Panel report, Prescott announced in March 2000 that he was rejecting both SERPLAN's original recommendations and the Panel's amendments. He reiterated that he was moving away from 'old style predict and provide' and was opting instead for a 'more flexible and responsive approach based on planning, monitoring and managing' (DETR, 2000a). The meaning of this phrase was spelled out in the revised version of PPG3 (Housing) which was published at the same time as the new policy for the south east region. It stipulated that housing provision should be monitored regularly, with the overall level of provision subject to continuous review (DETR 2000b).

By pursuing the policies laid down in PPG 3 in the south east it was argued in the government's response to the EiP Panel (DETR, 2000d p.12) that a key feature of RPG should be the 'concentration of development in urban areas', a policy that 'needs to be accompanied by action to secure a true urban renaissance in all the Region's urban areas'. The 'plan, monitor and manage' approach will facilitate 'a higher dwelling provision than proposed by SERPLAN and the local authorities... without increasing land take' (DETR, 2000d p.47). It was also proposed that there is no need to provide the full number of new homes specified by the EiP Panel. The rationale for providing a lesser figure than the 1.1 million specified in the Panel Report (and the housing projections) is not made clear in the government's response, although some explanation was provided in a Technical Advice Note published by the Government Office for the South East (GOSE, 2000). This latter document argues that some of the assumptions underlying the Panel's figure are questionable (e.g. levels of unmet demand) but it gives no clear and transparent explanation for undercutting the household projections. It says that government has followed a 'precautionary approach in providing a level of housing provision which is sufficiently realistic as a basis for testing through the plan, monitor and manage approach and therefore responsive to future trends in need' (*ibid.* p.11). Thus, John Prescott was convinced that only 43,000 new dwellings will be needed per annum between 1996 and 2016.

These figures were ultimately incorporated into RPG 9 (*South East*) in 2001. This document states:

> Recent housing completions in [the south east outside London] have averaged about 39,000 dwellings a year...the rate of completions should be increased in future years. However, until assessments have been completed of the capacity of urban areas and the scope for the potential growth areas to accommodate additional development, it is premature to specify precisely the increased level of provision and how it might be distributed, although it would be expected to result in around 43,000 dwellings a year. Future development needs to be achieved without perpetuating the trend to more dispersed and land-extensive patterns of development...It should be possible, through a plan-led process, to provide more dwellings than have been provided in recent years with proportionately less impact on land and other resources (GOSE, 2001 pp.47-48).

We quote this extract at length because it illustrates how the government is trying to 'square the circle' in the south east: it seeks to provide a projected number of dwellings (although less than the national projections stipulate are needed) while simultaneously downplaying the spatial impact of the figures. It can only justify this move by arguing that the 'required amount' of housing in the region should be delivered in 'a sustainable way' (GOSE, 2001 p.53). This means providing as much of this housing as possible in urban areas (in line with PPG 3). In this, as in general planning policy, the government is seeking to improve its rural credentials. In so doing, it is bolstering the rationality of sustainable planning with the consequence that overall levels of required housing may not be met (see Holmans, 2001).

Conclusion

We see here that planning for housing has traditionally been conducted via a hierarchical top-down structure in which the central state constructs forecasts of demand and then ensures that local planning authorities act within the framework that these demand considerations require. In the main, the alignment of agencies within this planning sector is achieved through the use of the housing projections. As a form of governmentality, the housing projections work effectively because they are freed from local contexts. They extract characteristics from complex situations, 'combine' them, 'shuffle' them and 'aggregate' them in new representations of the socio-spatial world and allow government to 'act at a distance' on a whole variety of local agencies (including local planning authorities and local plan participants) (Latour, 1987). The housing projections are complex. They use such abstract categories as population, household, migration, cohorts, vacancy rates, and conversions in order to build up a comprehensive picture of demographic and household change. These categories are then placed within trends and extrapolated into future scenarios of population and household growth. Not only do the categories run along the 'smooth rails' provided by government agencies with their elaborate statistical techniques, but they also act to reinforce the connections, obligations and responsibilities that tie the various parts of the planning hierarchy together. This process of transportation works to ensure that the actions of planners at the local level are shaped in accordance with the perceived need (at the centre) for new housing.

However, the very success of this system in delivering housing to the local level is beginning to undermine its efficacy. Because the figures are seen to work effectively, they are thought to 'drive' the system; thus, opposition to extensive new development tends to focus upon the forecasting techniques that bring housing demand into the decision making system. This opposition attempts to push the figures 'off the rails' so that other considerations (such as the environment) come into play. One strategy has been to attempt to undermine the figures themselves, highlighting the uncertainties and inconsistencies that lie within the categories (see, for instance, Bate, 1999). Yet, while the projections are deemed to be inherently uncertain, they are also widely assumed to be the best projections currently available. Thus, a challenge to the status of the figures as adequate representations of the future has largely foundered (see the discussion in Breheny, 1999).

An alternative strategy has attempted to *spatialize* the figures; that is, efforts have been made - by environmental organizations, local residents and amenity groups - to place the numbers within a set of robust regional and local contexts so that their 'value' can be assessed alongside a host of competing considerations, notably stemming from the environmental impact of housing development. This approach was nicely summarized by Tony Burton, when speaking for the CPRE in front of the House of Commons Environment Select Committee:

> What we need to do is factor into the equation all those other demands that society has and those needs that society has, be they social needs or be they environmental needs; and we must have a much more rounded view of where we are going, of which housing development is just one part (House of Commons, 1995 p.141).

This more 'rounded view' would require the spatial contextualization of the projections. No longer should they 'hover' over regional and local contexts, descending only to prescribe a set of developmental actions; for the CPRE, a new approach, one that gives 'equal consideration to the environmental capacity of different areas' should be introduced to replace the 'top-down, demand-led approach' (*ibid.*). In important respects, the Labour government's policy amendments seem to largely accord with the CPRE view, as the example of SERPLAN and south east regional planning indicates. SERPLAN effectively sought to embed the planning projections firmly in the environmental capability of the region. In so doing it effectively ensured that a specific and particular development trajectory was outlined and that the projections would not be met.

These amendments to policy will alter the status of the housing projections, as Allinson (1999 p. 112) puts it:

> the feeling is that forecasts will be based on how much housing an area can absorb rather than how much its past trends indicate it will need. Ultimately, policy making may depend on who defines an area as "full" (the government? the local councils? house builders?) and whether the solution lies in an autocratic authority or compromise.

In the next two chapters we investigate further the consequences of 'bringing the figures down to earth' and show that different actors have different definitions of 'capability', 'capacity', 'need', 'demand' and 'sustainable development'. As these various claims are made within the local plan reviews, they underline the potential complexity of the decision-making process in planning for housing and they provoke the following question - how are the various claims to be assessed against each other? In other words, what should be the over-arching goal of the policy?

Local debates must be structured in line with a clear set of policy objectives. Yet, too often in the past the structuring process has overridden the local debates. In moving away from this tight mode of structuration, the danger arises, however, that no clear policy momentum may emerge, leading to divergent policy outcomes in different regional and local contexts. Material presented in the following chapters shows that, while the assertion of local discretion can facilitate a richer debate over development options at the local level, it also runs the risk of delivering the worst of both worlds - no overall strategy but local frustrations at the limited nature of the debates. We raise these issues in the course of a discussion of how the housing figures became immersed in two local plans - a structure plan and a district plan. These plans belong to an area - Buckinghamshire - in which the growth in new houses has been high in recent years. Thus, the debate around the numbers was expected to be intense. We outline the character of these debates in the context of the two development plan reviews and draw out some general lessons for the conduct of a newly spatialized planning for housing system.

Chapter 5

Competing Rationalities in Structure Planning

Introduction

Previous chapters have considered the structure of planning policy and the changing nature of that policy. We have argued that two main rationalities of planning have been competing with one another over the last twenty years or so: one, concerned with development, seeks to align planning with the 'market' and gives developers considerable freedom of manoeuvre; the other, concerned with environment, asserts the need to place development in complex spatial or territorial contexts, so that a whole range of (economic, social, environmental) criteria are used to evaluate particular planning decisions or policies. These two rationalities imply differing policy structures: according to the first, policy should be formulated centrally and then disseminated throughout the policy framework; according to the second, differing agencies, located at various spatial scales, should have a say in policy development so that territorial complexity is made more central to policy formulation and implementation. In the previous chapter we considered the impact of these two rationalities on the policy structure in planning for housing.

We turn our attention here to planning in the arena of the county and examine how planners at this tier of government attempt to 'balance' the two rationalities against each other. We thus concentrate upon competing discourses of growth and environmental protection in an actual case of plan preparation. The forum in which we examine these discourses is the Buckinghamshire County Structure Plan. As various commentators have noted (e.g. Counsell, 1998; 1999), structure plans are an arena in which a whole host of competing concerns associated with development, environment, social equity and so on, come to be played out. Analysis of the debates circulating around and through planning at this level will help show how the two rationalities affect actual planning processes at the local scale, and will help us to consider the implications of embedding policy in given spatial contexts.

In particular, it will enable us to examine how participants combine strategic and local concerns. The structure plan is a useful context in which to do this as it must provide a strategic overview of development patterns in the county, but in a way that pays heed to the impact on particular local areas. Although structure plans have traditionally been seen as too abstract to be of much interest to local participants, this situation has changed with the introduction of the plan-led approach. Many local activists have quickly realized that policies encoded at this level will later serve to configure more local policies and development-control decisions (Abram *et al.*, 1996). Thus, they have begun to actively engage with the structure plan review processes. Our study is situated in the mid-1990s when this realization was first becoming evident. The results thus enable us to see, firstly, what local level participation aims to achieve and, secondly, how this participation is configured by national and regional policies.

We firstly provide some background information on the Buckinghamshire study area (see Figure 5.1). This area, which is situated in an economic 'hot spot', has seen some of the most rapid growth in England, and continues to experience acute housing pressure. However, this location creates a number of contradictions, for alongside the rapid in-migration of highly-educated and highly-resourced residents has come a strengthening of defensive discourses about the environment and a more organized approach toward local representation in policy-making. Local sensitivity to planning issues has become heightened as the composition of the local population, especially in the rural areas, has altered (Murdoch and Marsden, 1994; Chapter 2 above). This sensitivity has been increasing during the 1980s and 1990s, notably following the rows around housing in the south east in the late 1980s and mid-1990s. The county thus provides an excellent context in which to consider the competing aspirations of local 'stakeholders' and their potential impact on policy.

We examine how these aspirations came into conflict as the review process unfolded. We firstly consider how the plan was put together by the county planners and the assumptions that were incorporated into its core policies. We show how the plan both shaped, and was itself shaped by, the discourses of development and environment that ran through the review. Both discourses came quickly to the fore: on the one hand, developers were concerned to ensure that the housing figures were implemented in full (in fact they tried to get these numbers increased) so as to maximize the scope for development; on the other hand, environmentalists and local residents sought to undermine the figures and to restrict the amount of likely development, mainly by asserting a form of rural protectionism. We show how the contest between the two discourses was enacted, paying particular attention to the role of developers in pushing the numbers into the plan (the environmental discourse will be examined more extensively in the next chapter).

The account is based on a period of fieldwork carried out by the authors in 1994-1995. This fieldwork consisted of a study of responses to Buckinghamshire County's Draft Structure Plan, a series of semi-structured interviews with respondents, and participant observation at the Examination in Public (EiP) held in November 1994. We examined how the two main discourses of development and environment were constructed and followed the arguments as they were put

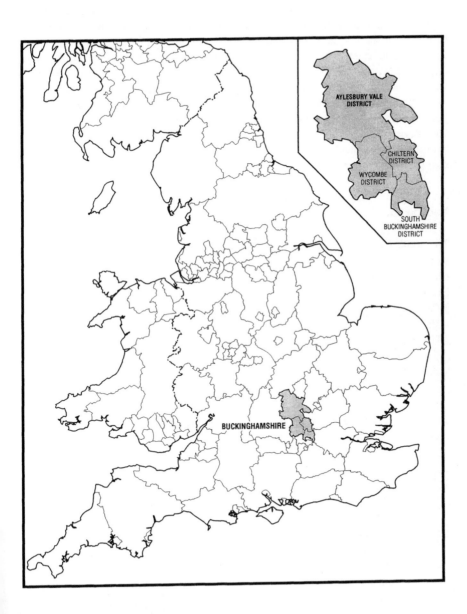

Figure 5.1   Map of the Buckinghamshire study area

forward by different groups and actors. We also attempted to define whose views proved most influential in the formulation of the policies.

In presenting our findings here we aim to show that when local planning policy becomes embedded in spatial contexts it also becomes embedded in the networks of planning relations that configure those contexts. In the case presented here we can see two networks in competition: on the one hand, a 'preservationist' alliance, held together by the rationality of environmental protection; on the other, a loose network of developers seeking to enhance the scope for development. As we shall see, both these networks had some impact on planning policy outcomes in the county but the activities of both were inextricably bound up with national policy; the groups both reflected that policy and promoted it within the structure plan review. At the local level, the national and the local become intertwined (Murdoch and Marsden, 1995). The important point to investigate is which tier ultimately determines policy outcomes.

Buckinghamshire in context

The south east is the core economic region of the UK: not only does London, a world city, cast a giant shadow over the region, but many of the most powerful economic and political institutions are located in the area (Allen *et al.* 1998). These characteristics ensure a degree of almost permanent economic buoyancy. This is reflected in the region's continued economic dominance of the rest of the UK; for instance, London and the south east accounts for around one third of the country's GDP. The buoyancy of the area is also evident from its business structure which is oriented towards the most dynamic sectors of the economy, as can be seen from Table 5.1:

Table 5.1   Economic activity in the south east (percentage of employees by sector in 1997)

	SE	UK
Agriculture	2.3	2.1
Mining	0.3	0.8
Manufacturing	20.5	26.0
Construction	5.1	6.1
Distribution	22.6	19.9
Transport	9.1	8.7
Finance	19.9	15.9
Edu/social	9.3	9.2

Source: Regional Trends, 1998.

The region has a much lower proportion of its workforce in extractive and manufacturing industries than the UK as a whole but a much higher proportion in areas such as distribution and finance. The service-based nature of the south eastern economy accounts in part for its success but does not imply that this economy is immune to recession, as the downturn in the late 1980s and early 1990s showed. It does mean, however, that many employees in the region tend to be in some of the best paid, most dynamic sectors as Table 5.2 indicates:

Table 5.2   Average weekly earnings in the south east (£ in 1997)

	Males	Females	All
SE	428.3	306.5	382.5
UK	407.3	286.2	366.3

Source: Regional Trends, 1998.

The buoyancy of the regional economy has traditionally resulted in low levels of unemployment and in 1997 only 3.3% of the region's workforce were so classified (compared to 4.4% in the UK as a whole - Regional Trends, 1998), while economic activity rates for both men and women are traditionally above the national norm.

The high levels of employment in the region have bolstered a relatively high degree of in-migration from other regions of the UK. During the first half of the 1980s, for instance, the southern half of England (including the south east, the south west, East Anglia and the East Midlands) gained on average around 50,000 people per year from the rest of England, although this number fell during the later years of the decade coinciding with the economic slowdown of the late 1980s and early 1990s (Atkins *et al.*, 1996). The south east continually recorded high levels of in-migration, although this also slowed towards the end of the decade: for instance, in 1996, 228,000 people moved into the area (Regional Trends, 1998). These trends ensured constant pressure for development and put particular pressure on the housing market.

There are two notable features of the regional housing market: firstly, levels of owner occupation are higher in the south east than elsewhere - in 1996, 74 per cent of dwellings in the region were owner-occupied compared to 67 per cent nationally; secondly, house prices in the south east are markedly higher than in the rest of the country, with the average price for a house in the region standing in 1997 at £97,739 compared to £79,732 in England and Wales as a whole (Regional Trends, 1998). The price of houses in the region, linked to the high level of owner occupation would seem to bear out Ray Forrest's (1987 p.1629) comment that 'the owner-occupied market in the south east... is becoming a closed shop, an exclusive club with escalating membership costs'.

Tony Fielding (1992) has thus proposed that the movement of population in and out of the region is structured along the lines of social class (see also Savage *et al.*, 1993). He introduces the notion of the south east as an 'escalator region'. Noting that the region, with its dynamic economy, offers rich opportunities for social promotion and the creation of middle-class careers, Fielding argues that young middle-class adults will be drawn to the area from regions which are notably lacking in such opportunities: 'young adults will tend to gravitate towards the former and away from the latter. Older people, some of them in-migrants as young adults, will tend to migrate away from the former towards the latter' (Fielding 1998, p.49). However, while young, well-educated workers tend to be mobile, and therefore able and willing to seek out good jobs in dynamic regions, by the time they reach middle age they express a desire to move away from the most dynamic urban areas towards smaller towns and settlements, both within and beyond the south east. The region therefore acts as a 'social escalator', allowing young adults to move into the middle class while sending established middle-class members to other areas.

While people in middle-class careers are drawn to dynamic labour markets and urban locations early in their working lives, Fielding's notion of the escalator indicates that they begin to move away from urban locations to smaller towns, free standing settlements and villages as they approach middle age. As we noted in Chapter 2, this movement seems to be associated with a variety of factors including disapproval of urban life (pollution, stress, crime and so on, particularly problematic for people with young families) and a yearning for some kind of rural idyll.

Champion *et al.*'s (1998) research on the 1991 census highlights that the people leaving metropolitan areas for the countryside are tending to move from the 'well to do' suburbs of London, especially those located along the western, northern and southern boundaries of the city. Areas such as Hillingdon, Hounslow, Enfield and Sutton recorded the largest net migratory losses to non-metropolitan areas. Given that these areas tend to suffer least from the acute urban problems that seem so unpalatable to many city dwellers, Champion *et al.* are forced to conclude that the pro-rural 'pull' aspects of counterurbanization prevail over anti-urban 'push' aspects. They argue that

> all the evidence seems to suggest that there is a deep force in the English psyche which is driving people to aspire to a rural lifestyle' for 'very few people appear to be forced to make [a counterurbanizing] move, either by their employers or by the conditions prevailing in the places that they have moved from (1998 p.31).

They imply that the lure of the English countryside seems to override any prevailing anti-urbanism in accounting for counterurbanization in the south east. Given the attractiveness of the countryside, it seems more than likely that its preservation will be of concern to these new rural residents.

However, these theories about the 'English psyche' ignore two further elements that we believe have been significant influences on counterurbanizing trends. One of the major 'pull' factors for those moving out of desirable suburbs of London, in particular, has been the differential in property prices. While the value of rural residences has escalated, they have not kept the same hectic pace as property prices within London, and a number of residents in the case study village (see chapter 6), for example, indicated that rather than be priced into less desirable suburbs of London, they would seek the equivalent 'quality of life' and more floor space in a village or small town outside the capital. Metropolitan railway and underground lines extend a significant distance out of the city, making commuting times proportionally comparable with outer London suburbs. At the time of fieldwork, the market value of a 3-bedroomed terraced house in Ealing, say, was more than that of a four-bedroomed detached house in villages such as that discussed in our case study in the next chapter.

In addition, counterurbanizers who have moved into the city from other parts of the country may to some significant extent have moved from other rural or semi-rural districts, and rather than being drawn by some psychological obsession with a form of rural nationalism (or national ruralism), find that life in London is more stressful than they initially assumed. Some proportion of counterurbanizers, are, we suggest, moving *back* to the country, rather than moving *to* an imagined idyll.

In addition, we might suggest that the protectionism of rural villages is informed historically by the developments of the post-war period, not all of which were successful in hindsight. Rural residents in Aylesbury Vale, for example, and in other parts of Buckinghamshire, rue the transformation of Aylesbury town during the 1970s. during this period, the town was transformed from a small, 'characterful' and 'traditional' market town into a concrete-dominated modern hub, and many residents described this process as the 'ruination' of Aylesbury (see figure 5.2 for an illustration of the visual effects of these changes). Thus, rural preservationists often lack any confidence in the building and architectural industries to offer development that enhances particular places, rather than expanding towns according to non-place-specific blueprints. Thus, preservationists are not only concerned with the retention of 'middle-class privilege', nor anti-urbanism, but are also concerned about the loss of unique-ness of place, or, in other words, about loss of place-identity.

The effects of a buoyant economy and social trends which place a high status on living in the countryside combine to put many rural areas - especially those located in the more affluent areas of the region such as to the south, north and west of London - under a great deal of pressure and demand remains high for some kind of access to rural space, whether for leisure or living purposes. Situated in the north western part of the south-east region, the rural areas and small towns of Buckinghamshire are a key destination for many of those people moving out of greater London and other cities, and those moving to the city for employment, but not attracted by city-living. Population growth in the county has been particularly intense - between 1971 and 1991 Buckinghamshire had the fastest population increase in the UK, (around 10 per cent) and rates have remained high since.

The county has a long tradition of middle-class in-migration to the rural areas (Murdoch and Marsden, 1994). As the south east as a whole - particularly those counties to the west and north of London - has seen a growth in this social strata so the most attractive environments in Buckinghamshire have witnessed a continued in-migration of wealthy residents, particularly into the preserved southern districts. Murdoch and Marsden suggest that villages in the county are becoming increasingly 'middle class' in character. For instance, they find, on average, that around two-thirds of village residents have moved into their houses within the last ten years and that almost half of all rural residents fall into socio-economic groups 1, 2 and 3, with a further third in the economically inactive (retired) category. Almost all the residents in these villages showed themselves to be strongly opposed to further development with the vast majority (70-80 per cent) wishing not to see more new homes or development opportunities in the local countryside (see Murdoch and Marsden, 1994, especially Chapter 2).

Plate 5.1   Buckinghamshire County Hall, Aylesbury, and County Library approach (Photo S Abram 1997)

Following an analysis of development trends in Buckinghamshire, Murdoch and Marsden (1994 p.xi) propose that in comparable areas of high growth great efforts will be made to protect rural and environmental features. They suggest an 'ideal type' - the 'preserved countryside' - to capture the nature of the interaction between development and restraint:

the preserved countryside ... is perhaps evident throughout the English lowlands, as well as in attractive and accessible upland areas, and is characterized by anti-development and preservationist attitudes and decision making. Such concerns are expressed mainly by new social groups in the countryside, such as middle-class fractions who may impose their views through the planning system on would-be developers. In addition, demand from these fractions provides the basis for new development activities associated with leisure, industry and residential property. The reconstitution of rurality is often highly contested by articulate consumption interests who use the local political system to protect their positional goods (see also Marsden *et al.*, 1993).

This countryside 'type' was formulated very much with rural areas in Buckinghamshire in mind. The county illustrates the workings of the 'preserved countryside' because it is located within an economically dynamic region but will be used as a place of 'retreat' (Lowe *et al.*, 1995) or 'escape' (Bell, 1994) by affluent ex-urbanites; the function of rural Buckinghamshire will therefore be to provide an 'outlet' from the increasingly frenetic urban world that so often accompanies rapid economic growth. And, as more and more people turn away from the city so they will seek to protect the areas that facilitate this 'escape'; they will seek to preserve rurality in the face of increasing (urban) pressure and will endeavour to steer development into other locations (Charlesworth and Cochrane, 1994). Our fieldwork has also indicated that the 'new' middle-classes migrating into the rural South East may find allies with the existing middle class rural residents, whose attitudes to development have become less enthusiastic in light of the changes that post-war developments have brought.

Essentially, Murdoch and Marsden (1994) propose that, in the wake of counterurbanization, a 'middle-class countryside' is gradually coming into being in places such as rural Buckinghamshire. Partly through their dominance of rural institutions (such as local councils and community groups), and partly through their willingness to mount political campaigns against development, members of the middle-class are gradually 'winning out' in the battle for rural space. In the process, other claims on rural space, whether from powerful developers, working-class residents, urban youth, or travelling people, are being sidelined. Essentially, a cumulative process of class composition has been set in train (Savage *et al.*, 1993), for as preservationism succeeds in excluding 'other' forms of development so it excludes 'other' people (one mechanism being house prices: as fewer houses are built at the same time as demand for a rural home rises so price inexorably rise pushing country dwellings beyond the means of all but the most affluent).

Other authors have challenged this view. Keith Hoggart (1997), for instance, takes issue with the whole idea of the countryside as 'middle-class territory' (as proposed by Murdoch, 1995) and argues that there is far less evidence than might be imagined for such an assumption. In particular, he proposes that there is a great deal of spatial variation in the composition of the middle class - notably between urban fringe and more remote rural districts - so that a fair amount of sensitivity is needed when applying notions such as 'middle-class capture' to any particular rural area. He believes we cannot assume that increasing numbers of middle-class residents give rise to common socio-economic outcomes. Referring to the political activities of this social formation, Hoggart (1997 p.259) argues that:

> The opposition of village residents to particular developments is very real but highly constrained. Better organized and more powerful players than the amorphous, service classes influence procedures, regulations and structures in the countryside...It might well be that the service classes do not want growth in their locality but *ceteris paribus* there is little evidence that localized groups are capable of successfully resisting development when these are supported by powerful national interests....

Hoggart appears to be suggesting here that to talk of middle-class dominance is misplaced for such dominance can be undermined by the activities of 'powerful' national actors. As previous chapters above have shown, there is considerable evidence to support this point: it is abundantly clear that developmental actors do frequently override local aspirations, even when these aspirations are forcefully presented by articulate middle-class groups. Importantly, Hoggart's argument indicates that, rather than characterizing the 'preserved countryside' as simply a 'middle-class space', it is perhaps appropriate to investigate the consequences of locality-based contests between extra-local development actors and local, middle-class anti-development actors.

The bulk of this chapter is therefore given over to pursuing this theme and we attempt here to tease out how this economic and social context intermeshes with the competing rationalities outlined earlier. We seek to understand how the positional status of the 'preserved countryside' is under continual assault e.g. precisely because these areas are so popular with counterurbanizing groups they are also targetted by developers seeking to capitalize on the huge gains that can be made if housing development is steered through the planning process. Therefore, the anti-development activists have to remain vigilant and must continually involve themselves in planning (at all levels). Yet, developers are also involved in these arenas. Thus, planning in places such as Buckinghamshire is constantly buffeted between the demands of developers and the demands of the preservationists. In order to understand how processes of regulation seek to adjudicate between the conflicting demands we examine how these trends appear in practice in one arena of contestation - the structure plan.

Planning in Buckinghamshire

Prior to the recent local government review (which took effect after the events to be described below) Buckinghamshire was made up of five districts: Milton Keynes and Aylesbury Vale in the north; High Wycombe, South Bucks and Chiltern in the south. The initial growth centre was High Wycombe where, during the 1960s, the Labour controlled council sanctioned a policy of substantial public housing investment. However, by the early 1970s a coalition of conservation groups, spearheaded by the local branch of the CPRE and the Chilterns and High Wycombe amenity societies, forced the adoption of a much more restrictive growth policy in the south of the county, an area which comprises mainly of Green Belt and Area of Outstanding Natural Beauty.

Over the following two decades, these restrictive policies came to be reinforced: early rounds of structure planning, for instance, effectively entrenched containment in the south and urban expansion in the north of the county. The plans, in turn, came to be bolstered by an enhanced local political coalition - made up of amenity societies, action groups, local residents, county and district councillors - which sought to ensure no incursion of development into the rural areas in both the south and the north of the county. As Charlesworth and Cochrane (1994 p.1732) put it:

> There appears to be a mutual understanding between the local planners and local residents of the need to retain strict planning policies and withstand pressures for development. Indeed, this can be seen as a mutually beneficial (and particularly powerful) alliance in which the traditional development control activities of planners are justified by the activity of local groups.

This coalition - which had effectively consolidated itself around the rationality of 'environmental protection' (see Murdoch *et al.*, 1999) - only accepted growth in the urban areas of Aylesbury and Milton Keynes, and to a lesser extent High Wycombe, and sought to ensure that development plan policies adhered to these protectionist principles. Further growth was, therefore, pushed into the north of the county, notably the town of Aylesbury and the new town (later city) of Milton Keynes.

Whilst house builders and developers worked tirelessly against this coalition (as their aim was to increase development in the desirable and lucrative areas of the rural south of the county), it was supported by groups such as the Chamber of Commerce, not least because they believed Buckinghamshire's rural countryside to be a positive factor in the attractiveness of the area to employers. It should be noted, also, that the ruling political groups of both county and district during this early coalition phase were Conservatives, whose strongholds were in the rural areas, particularly the south of the county, in contrast to the higher Labour presence, particularly in Milton Keynes and Buckingham.

In what follows, we investigate how this coalition operated within the review of the Structure Plan (which took place in the first half of the 1990s) in order to see whether it could still impose itself on county-level policy. Given that the plan was being formulated in a context where further rapid growth looked certain (the latter stages of the review coincided with the 4.4 million debate discussed earlier), it seemed likely that a sharp contest between protectionists and developers would ensue. In particular, many of those residents who had moved into the rural villages during the preceding two to three decades (for reasons outlined in Chapter 2) became concerned that another round of house building was set to take place in the county. However, developers were well aware that the housing projections carried great weight in the review process and were keen to ensure that they were implemented in full. The Buckinghamshire Structure Plan thus became a key arena for debates about the future development of the county. By following its development we therefore illustrate what happens when a rationality of development runs up against a rationality of the environment in a given spatial context.

Positioning the plan

The review of the Structure Plan began at the end of 1990. It was initiated by a group of planning officers who put together a series of papers on the contemporary state of Buckinghamshire, in terms of housing, employment and transport. They also summarized national policies and PPGs (particularly significant at this time was the opening up of the 'East Thames Corridor', an effort to regenerate areas to the east of London which it was hoped would be effective by the latter part of the plan period thereby taking pressure off counties in the north and west of the region). The summary papers and survey results were then submitted to the County Structure Plans and Local Plans Panel. The Panel comprised of ten county councillors, providing the member input to the review process. The culmination of this initial process was a synthesis of all the available information from a multitude of sources. This information was translated into what was called a Baseline Strategy, which summarized all the elements which would be included in the new Structure Plan. It is important to note however, that the strategy, while only a provisional outline of Structure Plan policies, also stood as a position statement on the part of the political members of the Council. According to a planning officer involved in this process, the members were concerned to ensure that the south of the county - the Green Belt and the Chilterns Area of Outstanding Natural Beauty (AONB) - remained sacrosanct: 'they've always made clear right from the word go that they wanted the Green Belt protected and they wanted the AONB protected. You've got those two fixed starting points which they were firmly attached to' (interview). In other words, the Panel comprised a key part of the preservationist coalition mentioned above. This indicates that the decisions on the spatial dispersal of development taken during earlier phases of strategic planning had become entrenched, not just in planning policies, but in the networks of actors surrounding the review.

In fact, this objective of rural protection, which was formulated right at the start of the review, was virtually adopted wholesale from the previous version of the Structure Plan. Moreover, RPG bolstered this starting point as protection of Green Belt and AONB were firmly entrenched at this time in the regional guidance policies. The policy on protection of the south was thus consolidated early on in the plan review process. These decisions set the parameters for all subsequent arguments.

Having arrived at the starting point for the plan, the County Council circulated the Baseline Strategy to the district authorities (Milton Keynes, Aylesbury Vale, South Bucks, Chiltern and Wycombe) and a series of meetings between these agencies ensued. With the enhanced importance of the development plan in the new post-1991 plan-led regime, the districts recognized that they should be involved quite closely in the review process. The district planners sought to add their more local concerns into the proposed policy mix. In particular, they were involved in the adoption of the housing figures and their distribution throughout the county. These numbers were derived from the (then) DoE projections which were agreed by the counties (within the context of the regional planning forum) using the districts' calculations of available housing land. The county's regional housing quota stood at 62,600 and regional planners specified that this number of additional dwellings should be provided within Buckinghamshire during the period 1991-2011.

While there was a remarkable degree of consensus between the various local authorities over the initial policy statement, some difference in emphasis between the southern districts and those in the north could be detected. The Baseline Strategy, to maintain the Green Belt and AONB boundaries in the south - and thus focus development activity in the north of the county around Milton Keynes and Aylesbury - was welcomed by the southern districts of Chiltern and South Bucks. The northern districts went along with this approach, but they had reservations about the attitude of the southern districts. The northern districts were attempting to provide for substantial amounts of new development (theoretically, at least) to take the pressure off the south of the county, yet the latter authorities seemed to entertain little hope of providing anything at all. As a planner in Aylesbury Vale said to us during interview:

> I think South Bucks or Chiltern are planning to build 18 houses a year. I mean, that's not planning in my mind [laughs]. And there's Milton Keynes and ourselves and we're talking about thousands, tens of thousands and, you know, somebody's talking about 18 a year!

The Baseline Strategy, therefore, held together some rather tense and precarious alliances.

The adoption of policies oriented to protecting rural areas (especially in the Green Belt) was also bolstered by government policy on development plans, especially a new version of PPG 12 published in early 1992, which emphasized the need to ensure that development and growth are 'sustainable'. This was interpreted by both County and districts to mean that new houses should be built in existing settlements, near public transport access, and near employment areas, rather than in areas of say, open countryside, or where cars would provide the only means of transport for new residents. In other words, the interpretation of 'sustainability' in Buckinghamshire focused mainly (in fact, almost exclusively) on attempts to reduce residents' dependence on private cars. This was seen to be attainable through forward planning. Since access to public transport is concentrated in built up areas, and local government does not have powers to provide new public transport services, the County and districts concluded that new housing should be built in areas that already had public transport services (namely buses or trains), and that balancing homes and jobs meant that new employment sites should be located close to new housing land allocations. Although planners recognized that their powers to produce 'sustainable development' in practice were very limited, they believed that the best means of enabling others to develop sustainably was to concentrate development in areas with existing services.

Thus, the prevailing policy of restraint in the south, and concentration of development in Aylesbury and Milton Keynes in the north, received further legitimization: it was now couched in terms of 'sustainable development' and the need to discourage commuting. Once this strategy was adopted, other policies naturally followed. The housing distribution figures allocated the vast bulk of new housing to Milton Keynes, Aylesbury and High Wycombe. On employment policy, the plan stated that most new economic development would take place in the north 'with a greater emphasis on restraint in the constrained south' (Buckinghamshire County Council 1994a p.41). Milton Keynes and Aylesbury were identified as the main employment growth centres. In the rural areas *outside* the Green Belt, 'small scale employment-generating developments appropriate to... local needs... will normally be acceptable' (*Ibid.* p.42). Following on from this, it was stated that 'the impact of new development on the Bucks countryside will be reduced as much as possible' (*Ibid.* p.77). An increased priority was also attached to redeveloping urban land. Thus, the whole thrust of the plan was in accordance with the overriding need to protect the south of the county. While some in the north of the county were alarmed about the scale of development anticipated in Aylesbury Vale they did not dispute the strategy to protect the Green Belt and AONB, particularly in the light of a stated commitment to also protect rural areas in the north.

Public consultation

Once the consultation draft of the plan was produced, the County Council prepared for the task of involving the 'general public' in debate about the strategy. Accompanying publication of the consultation draft was a newspaper, produced in a tabloid style, 'which was a sort of simple layman's guide to what it was all about' as a planning officer said during interview. Approximately 100,000 copies of the paper were produced and distributed throughout the county in shopping centres, libraries, community centres and so on. Advertisements, alerting the public to the plan, were placed in local newspapers and a travelling exhibition toured settlements in the county to demonstrate what the plan was seeking to do. A number of public meetings were also organized.

According to a county planning officer: 'there was a very wide coverage for the public consultation stage. We didn't just put an advert in the paper and publish the plan and say, "get on with it, chaps". We really made strenuous efforts to inform and involve people in the process by a wide number of different ways' (interview). This planning officer recognized that the coverage was not comprehensive, but felt that it was always going to be difficult to get responses to the abstract issues inherent in strategic planning. He explained that despite their efforts to involve more people in the consultation process and to publicize as widely as possible, there were logistical limitations:

> We had to keep it within manageable proportions. You know, our members' time is limited. We can't possibly hope to involve everybody who we might wish to involve, we have to just try to narrow down: we involve the districts, interests and so on. We would have like to have involved more; it was just the logistics and time that prevented us. At the consultation stage you might say "it's just consultation" but we did do far more than we were required to do at the consultation stage, you know, we really went out of our way to try and advertise the plan through every medium possible, to tell people what was going on, to solicit their views (interview).

The dissemination of information on the Structure Plan relied on a network of communication channels throughout the county, including libraries, community centres, parish councils and shopping centres, as well as certain pressure groups and agencies with whom the County Council were familiar. And in general the 'public' responses to the policies were supportive. Our interviews with a cross section of the respondents indicated that they were overwhelmingly concerned with protection of the physical environment, particularly the Green Belt and the rural areas of the north. Thus, they were supportive of the policy of restraint in the south and channelling development into Aylesbury and Milton Keynes. In other words, the preservationist coalition that had surrounded previous reviews seemed to be active during the present review.

The main objections to the strategy came, unsurprisingly, from the house builders. Their opposition derived from a desire to open up more development potential in the lucrative south of the county, notably by moving some of the allocations given to Milton Keynes down to Wycombe (demand for new houses was slack in Milton Keynes at the time of the review). For instance, one said: 'whilst accepting that a positive policy of placing emphasis of growth is required to alleviate perceived pressure in the South, the level of restraint is unacceptable and unrealistic' (interview). Another made the same point slightly more forcefully: '... restriction on development south of the Chiltern ridge is harmful...' (interview). We should stress, however, that the house builders were simply concerned with opening up opportunities for development in the constrained south; they were not at all preoccupied with over-development in the urban areas of the north, particularly

Aylesbury (as we shall see below, many believed Aylesbury could accommodate higher levels of development than the Structure Plan was then proposing).

At the consultation stage, however, the developers were unsuccessful. In replying to their complaints the County Council noted that three of the districts (Aylesbury Vale, Chiltern and Wycombe) were in agreement with their allocations, and South Bucks felt their allocation could not be accommodated without breaching Green Belt and AONB boundaries. In fact, the only change that was made at this time was a decrease in the overall number of dwellings (down from 62,600 to 61,700, due to a lower than expected number of completions in Milton Keynes and new information on post-2001household formation).

By the time the next version of the plan - the deposit draft - was published in April 1994, the principle of 'sustainable development' was very much in the foreground, with the chosen strategy being one of 'concentration and integration, rather than dispersal, with most new development located beyond the Green Belt and the Chiltern Hills in North and Mid Buckinghamshire' (Buckinghamshire County Council 1994b p.17). The plan claimed to distribute new dwellings using criteria such as:

> ...close correlation between jobs, community services and important local facilities, such as shops and schools ... the reduction of the need for car travel ....the protection of established planning constraints, such as Green Belts, Chilterns AONB, Heritage features, Sites of Special Scientific Interest and high grade farmland (Buckinghamshire County Council, 1994b pp.25-26).

The desire to protect the Green Belt and the AONB very quickly became wrapped up in the discourse of sustainability, and the main principles and broad strategy of the plan were couched in terms such as 'concentration', 'correlation' and 'integration'. Between 70-80 per cent of all housing proposed in the plan for the whole period would be sited in the three urban centres of Milton Keynes, Aylesbury and Wycombe. Thus, a rather more technical justification for the policy of southern preservation and concentration came to be employed. Ultimately, 'sustainable development' was seen to require upholding rather than undermining the Green Belt (this is line with Cullingworth's 1997a and b observations that sustainability criteria bolster planning's long-standing concern with protection).

At this stage in the review process the main principles had become entrenched. By stipulating right at the start that the Green Belt and AONB would be protected, the plan sought to ensure that the south would be little troubled by development. And, bolstered by the new discourse of sustainability, development in the north would, it was hoped, be steered into the two centres of Aylesbury and Milton Keynes. It seemed, therefore, that it would be difficult for actors opposed to the general aims of the plan, even if armed with extensive technical information, to simply undo the assumptions which lay at the heart of the strategy.

Discourses of development and environment at the Examination-in-Public

At this point in the review, the apparent interests of local residents were reflected in the geographic strategy. The desire on the part of both councillors (for political reasons) and planners (for professional reasons) to protect valued natural assets in the county had the support of those members of the public involved in the process (although we should note that there was a noticeable lack of interest in the review amongst the residents of Aylesbury, the town that was set to bear most of the new development). The main points of discussion had revolved around the distribution of development. A debate about housing numbers had yet to begin. The unease that many local residents and environmental groups felt about future levels of housing development only really began to become public at the EiP. In this forum, however, their views were to be set against those of the developers who seemed determined to get the numbers increased.

The EiP allowed a number of developers, conservationists, residents, planners, and other interested parties to debate the key issues in a roundtable discussion. The County Council and the EiP Chairman (who was invited to be chairman by the County, in negotiation with the Government Office of the South East), who was keen to allow anyone making major objections to the plan to participate, chose these participants. In effect, this meant that the EiP was dominated by developers, the constituent District Council planning officers, a handful of local residents' associations, and environmental groups. The EiP was not a broad-ranging discussion of the plan, however. All interjections were required to refer directly to stated policies within the draft plan; general issues concerning the conceptual or philosophical direction of the plan were ruled out of the debate by this strategy. Nevertheless, this forum gave each participant the chance to put forward their views on plan policies. From the arguments presented, we get an insight into the interests and goals of the key participants and the discursive strategies they employed to attain their goals.

The EiP took place in a conference centre owned by the County Council, a few miles out of Aylesbury town. The centre's location away from public transport access led to some ironic teasing about the Council's claimed commitment to sustainable transport policies, which added to a generally fairly light hearted but tense atmosphere. The parties sat around a large square arrangement of tables in a sequence that mirrored the 'discursive alliances' that subsequently developed, with council officers facing developers across the room, and other pressure groups between them and facing the Examination Panel (see Figure 5.2 below). Each participant had a small conference microphone in front of them on the table. The proceedings were recorded by the County Council, to be archived (although the recordings were not transcribed). When they were invited to speak, participants had to press a button on the microphone so that they would be heard, both in the room and on the recording, and a small red light came on as they did so. In his introduction, the Panel Chairman outlined the issues to be debated at the EiP, set the 'housekeeping' guidelines for how the Examination would run (on four days of each of three weeks with breaks for tea and lunch), and explained the microphone system. This latter instruction had to be repeated almost every day, to some general amusement, before it worked smoothly.

The first day of the EiP began with position statements from the various participants, and at this point the pressure groups and residents' groups were to the fore. The Chairman invited them to comment on five points, namely, growth, sustainability, the Green Belt, landscape, and rural communities. In so doing, they questioned the meaning of 'need' as opposed to 'demand' in relation to housing, forecasting based on past trends rather than current and future conditions, and the lack of a coherent rural policy. They called for housing forecasts based on 'need not greed'.

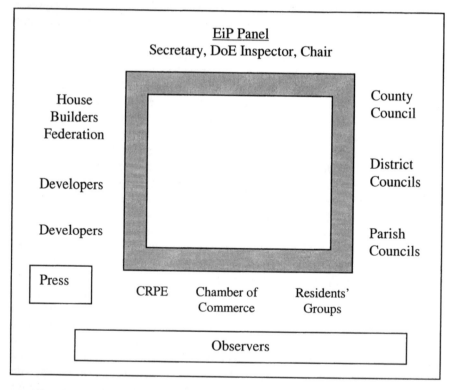

Figure 5.2   Arrangements at the Buckinghamshire EiP

Day two was dedicated to the housing figures, and was rapidly dominated by technical arguments between developers and Council demographers, with non-professional participants largely excluded from the discussion. The debate was technical, and included, for instance, a consideration of the vacancy rates used in the forecasting methods by both the County Council and the House Builders Federation. Some contributions from CPRE, parish councils and residents' groups were made, but they were couched in general terms about the distribution of housing. By and large, their comments were largely ignored by the other participants.

The developers used the EiP as a means of attacking many of the (preservationist) assumptions underlying the plan. Firstly, it became clear that if the house builders wished to increase the overall number of houses they would have to do so by undermining the housing projections; secondly, if they wished to alter the allocation, shifting some substantial number down into the south of the county where housing demand was more buoyant, they would have to ease the restrictions in the south. In order to do this they would have to point to inconsistencies, uncertainties and unwarranted assumptions in the general strategy and the policies of the plan.

In an implicit acknowledgement of the growing importance of the 'sustainable development' goal, the house builders attacked the geographic strategy by attempting to undermine the County Council's sustainability credentials. They noted that the Green Belt did not necessarily contribute to sustainable development and suggested that Green Belt control might be re-examined in relation to future development needs and the function of settlements enclosed within it.

The fact that the County Council had simply taken the Green Belt at face value, the HBF argued,

> has resulted in a situation whereby the development needs of the south of the county will not be met where they actually arise. People are expected to move or travel elsewhere to find new homes or jobs... The Federation therefore considers that the County Council's housing strategy is effectively a strategy of restraint, rather than any real attempt to address the County's future development needs in a more sustainable way. In these circumstances, the proposed strategy is self-defeating (HBF, 1994).

Planning consultants acting on behalf of both the house builders and landowners adopted a variety of strategies to destabilize the county's provisions. However, the goal was straightforward, as one planning consultant explained: 'they're obviously interested in the same thing, in pushing the numbers up, because if you push the numbers up there's a greater chance that any given site will then be able to come forward for housing' (interview). This participant was acting on behalf of a large landowner whose land he thought was suitable for both residential and industrial development. In order to increase the chances of the land being released for development, the consultant argued as follows:

> we were trying to persuade the panel that they ought to actually increase the number of dwellings in total for Bucks, that's the first bit of analysis that you do, you look at what figures they come up with, compare those with regional guidance to see how well they match, you look at the latest household projections to see whether or not in terms of household projections the

figures are still compatible. Usually county councils seek to allocate land for a lower figure than the regional guidance and certainly a lower figure than one would expect from household projections, so you're always arguing to push it up, from my perspective, you know, acting on behalf of a landowner or a house-builder (interview).

The County Council planning officers defended their figures as reflections of the national housing forecasts and as in line with regional guidance. In opposition to this, some developers argued that regional planning policy did not fix the housing figures, but provided only *guidance* which could be amended (or 'tested') at the EiP. Others claimed that household projections offered a maximum housing figure of 91,000, and the regional guidance figure, which stood at 65,000, comprised a *minimum* total. They argued that rather than follow the County's very cautious proposals, the EiP should find a figure somewhere in-between the two.

It was clear at this stage that the various developers were trying diverse strategies to undermine the County's housing figures, but not in any co-ordinated fashion. The HBF, for instance, took issue with the County Council's policy of accepting existing in-migration commitments up to 2006 and then only providing for 'natural increase' (i.e. with nil net in-migration) to 2011. This approach, the HBF argued, took no account of regional growth, the weakness of the west-east shift into the proposed East Thames Corridor development area, in-migration pressures, and the potential for job growth. The Federation provided a set of comparative figures and projections which gave alternative scenarios to those provided by the County Council. Putting particular emphasis on the mis-match between possible employment growth in the county and dwelling provision, the HBF plumped for a figure of 79,500 dwellings between 1991-2011, explaining that 'this is both realistic and reasonable, given the longer term intention to reduce growth'.

Other developers also arrived at the EiP with their own housing projections (ranging from 64,000 to 74,000) and attacked the County's figures using a number of arguments - the regional guidance figures were too low, there was an excessive and unrealistic reliance on the East-West shift, high levels of in-migration would continue, there was a mismatch between jobs and homes (linked to the issue of sustainability and the need to reduce commuting), and so on. Doubts were raised about the degrees of concentration and dispersal advocated in the plan, with certain developers arguing that the policies with regard to housing and employment were too restrictive. It was claimed that Aylesbury, of all the growth centres, had the potential to take a higher housing allocation, particularly as the town lies just beyond the Green Belt and AONB. The vacancy rates used by the County Council in their calculations were also criticised as too modest, thereby leading to a low overall figure.

Effectively the professional planning consultants and other representatives who spoke for the house builders were trying to open up the political dimensions of the plan to scrutiny through the mechanism of the numerical calculations presented.

For instance, on the housing figures, one representative of the house builders said to us that 'it's political pressure that is leading them to adopt the figure they have... It's the politics that leads to this' (interview).

The house builders employed their technical expertise in housing forecasts in order to open up the plan to changes in housing numbers. Their aim was to strengthen certain assumptions (the need for growth, for example) while undermining others (the need to protect the south). Other participants at the EiP were also hostile to certain elements of the plan in different ways. For instance, local village and environmental groups were concerned about overall levels of growth but they did not have the resources to formulate complex statistical arguments that were powerful enough to undermine the figures in the way that the house builders did. They appeared to make little impression, therefore, on the discourse of housing demand which dominated the EiP. The consultant mentioned above also stressed the amount of resources required to present demographic arguments persuasively:

> The biggest difficulty is that clients don't understand the amount of background work that's needed in order to put a case over properly because you need to do quite a lot of research. And if you can imagine, on household projections for example, the county will have done all sorts of computer modelling on household projections, the HBF will have commissioned somebody like the Chelmer Institute to do the same thing and if we go along, we won't have done any modelling... it can be very frustrating if you've not had sufficient funds from the client to do the work properly and you get there and you feel totally inadequate, you know, people are there and you think "what have I got to say?" (interview).

A two day debate on the assumptions incorporated in the use of housing projection models, hastily arranged at the end of the EiP, involved almost exclusively the County Council and the HBF. This debate had been requested by the Chairman earlier in the EiP when it became clear that the uses of statistical forecasting models had not been clearly explained. In particular, the respective uses of the Chelmer model for housing forecasts was brought into question. This became the defining issue, and effectively involved only the two participants with access to the model. The Panel Chairman commented later, in interview, that,

> Yes, the Chelmer model is a well respected model in demographic profiling circles and a lot of local authorities have used it. I found that the Chelmer model could be used to produce any figure at the end of the day. So, basically, the house builders wanted land, they may seriously and with integrity have felt that the 62,000 was ridiculously low, I don't know, there were no serious figures put forward for lower than 62. I think the CPRE put forward 54, but it wasn't seriously argued so I think 62 represented a floor figure (interview).

By 'seriously argued', the Chairman was referring to the use of specific statistical representations. The CPRE's arguments were loosely woven around the need for development to follow 'need' rather than 'demand' and the potential increase in tele-working (anticipating the rise in internet use). Despite his scepticism about the models, the Chairman was forced to conclude that the most cogent arguments derived from a discussion of the housing numbers. As he commented later, 'the whole business of number of dwellings provided that context of development versus anti-development, landscape protection versus the leftovers' (interview).

The arguments therefore revolved around numbers rather than around, for example, visions of a planned future for the county, transport issues, integration of services, or any other contemporary issues. As the consultant mentioned above indicated, influence over certain parts of the plan, such as housing numbers, is severely restricted:

> The bits that you can't influence without the technical expertise are the levels of growth, for example the number of dwellings that you're talking about. What you can argue about I think, is their distribution within a county (interview).

This comment indicates that the most significant topic in the EiP - levels of housing growth - was out of reach of the majority of participants. A technical discussion about forecasts and computer modelling was only possible for those who were engaged in such things, namely the HBF and the county planners. Despite the fact that many of the other participants had some amount of planning expertise (something which distinguishes them from most members of the 'general public') they were excluded from this discussion.

The CPRE representative, for example, had gained some planning knowledge by representing a village group (which we will meet briefly in the next chapter), but was essentially self-taught. She explained: 'I've just picked these things up in a rather haphazard way - I really am not an expert' (interview). Her main aim during the EiP, as she explained it, was

> principally trying to ensure that you don't get scattered groups of houses being built around the countryside....Very often you get farms right on the edges of the settlements and in those cases they can really simply be brought into the existing settlement and my feeling is there's no point getting excited about it. But if you get five houses suddenly being built just sort of scattered into the countryside then that's not what we really want (interview).

However, in order to present this argument, she had felt obliged to address demographic issues. She argued, in fact, that 'I think that we're in a terrible, terrible difficulty and....that is that to some extent it's becoming too technical'. As an instance of this she discussed the population increase in the south east in terms which showed both her familiarity with technical arguments and her inability to come to terms with the prevailing rationality:

> Why is the population increasing at 10 per cent every year in these counties? The total period fertility rate is slightly higher for Bucks than it is for England and Wales as a whole but it still is below the replacement level. So you cannot argue that it's local need....in the 1976 County Structure Plan, which I have...the low forecast was only exceeded in two of the districts across the county, but the overall outcome was 8 per cent below the low forecast. Now normally you take the median forecast when you're forecasting. If you took that, you'd be 12 per cent below the forecast. If the numbers that they come up with this time were 12 per cent below, then they would be looking for very many fewer additional sites for housing....There are no figures in the County Structure Plan for population - the only figures they've put in are for housing, and not only that, but the way in which they quote the figures varies, so sometimes they say you need x by 2006, y by 2011, but the only thing that they say all the time is that it at the end of the day is 61,700. Then you say how many people does this represent - the census says that there are 2.61 people per household so the only population figure you can have is by saying x times ... (interview).

Clearly the figures as found in the plan and used by other commentators were far from straightforward. Without access to complex statistical models, the local CPRE representative (who must be reckoned an especially experienced participant) could only present general queries over the assumptions based in the models. Most of her criticisms were presented during the EiP, but none were answered directly. Despite being a highly educated professional woman, she clearly felt disempowered by the procedures. As she commented,

> I suppose one is liable to be questioned about why one said things, but I think really all I can say is these figures really have to be looked at. What is the logic for saying that Bucks' population has to increase by 10 per cent in every decade? ...So all I hope is that they don't ask me too many questions - all I can do is to quote the figures from the census and things like that....

In a sense, the consultant reinforced this sense that participation is limited, claiming that, 'I don't think pressure groups actually affect what people like myself would be saying'. Moreover, although there were occasional surprises, he mostly found the different kind of pressure groups arguing predictably:

> the CBI turned up at that one as a pressure group, if you like, the local CBI for Bucks, and they were making points about the national economy and the importance of certain parts of Bucks and the need not to restrain growth and all that sort of stuff, and you would expect that. The CPRE turns up and

what they're talking about is not building on open land, you know, re-using existing urban land, and you'd expect them to say that...

Only when they were well resourced and presented clear arguments, he judged, were they effective at EiPs in terms of planning strategies:

> ...some of the Transport 2000 and people like that are very well organized, FoE are extremely well organized, and they come along and they say, I think, my own personal view, some very useful and sensible things. It depends what sort of axe they've got to grind, actually. If they've got a very narrow focus to why they're there, they will sometimes be of less value in a structure plan context than organisations that are a bit less focused but want to make general points, because that's really what it's all about. It's all about generalizations really.

This planning consultant here illustrates the difficulties of levels of abstraction within the planning hierarchy. He is reminding us that whereas arguments about local plans relate to sites - and are therefore tangibly linked to outcomes - the figures debated at the structure plan level remain abstract and undefined. These figures are not yet 'materialized', and will not become spatialized until the local planning stage (see Chapter 6). The strategic policies are effectively abstract, since they are not tied to spatial detail, and therefore become solid only through the use of numerical argument at the EiP. This abstraction is clearly easier for some participants to handle than others.

Outcomes

When it came to writing the report, the Panel Chairman commented that he had felt restricted to addressing the calculations over housing numbers according to the different uses of the models, rather than addressing the fundamental political assumptions included in the plan: 'There was an exercise to go through, a certain intellectual challenge to justify a figure and also to justify the allocations which went to each district. But after that the issues really fell into place' (interview). In other words, the whole plan and EiP report were largely driven by the discussion of the dwelling numbers. He also felt frustrated because discussion of the Green Belt and other *national* designations was beyond the remit of the examination, and recognized that these designations played a crucial role in conditioning the distribution of development. Moreover, he believed that the plan had failed to allocate the housing projections to particular geographic spaces in any meaningful way. Without allocating land to development, he argued, the planned dwellings remained notional, and the plan was incomplete. Once the figure is agreed, he suggested, it's then got to be allocated. It's not a question of, let's say we end up with a figure of plus 5,000, you can't then give each district council a thousand, I mean, you've got to argue, well some have to receive more than others. That was the interesting part, I think, of the report, certainly as far as writing up is concerned.

The balance of the arguments at the EiP was reflected in the report of the Panel. In other words, it dealt largely with *technicalities*. For instance, the report argued that the County Council had used a figure of 4.1 per cent vacancy rates for 1991 declining to 3 per cent in 2011. The Panel concluded that a rate nearer 4 per cent than 3 per cent would be more appropriate and calculated that a higher completion rate could be expected between 2001-2006. The total number of houses to be provided during the plan period was raised to 66,500. The house builders, through their deployment of technical arguments, had thus won a minor victory, despite making little or no impact on the spatial distribution of development.

Conclusion

The structure plan review had mixed results for local participants. On the one hand, the geographic strategy largely accorded with local aspirations as the Green Belt and rural areas were protected. The amount of participation from urban areas was low (particularly from Aylesbury) so those most affected by this strategy did not become involved in the review process. Whilst convenient for the Council planners, who were suggesting radical increases in housing provision particularly in Aylesbury, it was unfortunate for urban residents who we can only assume remained largely ignorant of the debate going on about the future of their local environments. However, commenting on this feature of structure plan participation, one planner suggested that people in Aylesbury Town were well aware of continued development, and were therefore not surprised by the planning consultation. In fact, as we shall see (in Chapter 6), it was the residents of rural villages around the fringes of Aylesbury who raised most objections to developments later specified in the local district plan, since despite development being directed towards 'existing settlements' such as Aylesbury, the scale of development proposed (increase by nearly a third) made it necessary to expand the town outwards into open countryside.

Yet, had residents of Aylesbury been present it must be doubtful whether they could have made much impact on the proceedings. There were two key issues up for discussion: the *distribution* of development and the *amount* of development. Decisions on the first of these had been taken right at the start of the review process so that the rural areas of north and south were granted protection. This decision was underpinned by a local anti-growth coalition as well as national planning policy. With the emergence of sustainability criteria it gained further strength. There was thus very little discussion of this issue at the EiP (although the HBF questioned the true 'sustainability' of Green Belt designations). The level of development, notably housing was also equally impervious to external influence. As we have seen above, the debate about housing numbers was technical and therefore exclusive. Even those local participants who had taken the trouble to participate could make little headway in the face of the informed arguments presented by developers and planners. Whenever they did attempt to mount a challenge their concerns were too easily characterized as 'parochial' or 'emotional'. Thus, the figures emerged in the Structure Plan pretty much unscathed.

The two outcomes on distribution and development levels thus reflected not only the rationalities of developmentalism and environmentalism but also the alliances in which these rationalities were embedded in at the local level. We can see that County Council planners were linked to planning consultants and developers such as the HBF through an adherence to the same technical discourse. This resulted in a set of housing numbers appearing in the plan. On the other side of the argumentative divide, local councillors were linked to local residents, environmental groups and planners by a shared appreciation of the need to protect rural spaces. The debate about distribution was dominated by this informal alliance. In the main, it was shaped by a discourse of sustainable development at the core of which lay rural protectionism. Between these two local policy networks there was little room for a third position, which might have been concerned with the 'quality of life' in urban locations.

We can also see from this case study how the different tiers are tied into the planning hierarchy. PPG criteria and the housing figures combined to ensure that development flowed into the county and was distributed according to the principles of 'sustainability'. These national policies flowed directly into the two local coalitions and legitimized their activities. The eventual outcome could be seen to reflect a congruence between strong national policy and robust local alliances.

In conclusion it is worth pointing out that the policies flowing into the county during this period (the mid-1990s) bore a passing resemblance to those now being strengthened at the national level by the Labour administration. Sustainability determined the distribution of houses so that urban areas looked set to bear the brunt of development (despite their high growth rates of recent times) in ways which are quite reminiscent of the latest version of PPG 3 (*Housing* – DETR, 2000b). Development in rural areas was kept to a minimum, and was in any case highly unpopular locally, meaning that local politicians would resist this approach (see next chapter). Recent policy pronouncements which attempt to further strengthen 'planning for sustainable development' (e.g. by developing 'brownfield first') can only reinforce these trends. While the new policies may lead to a downplaying of the projections, so that local arguments are given freer play, it looks as though these arguments will in any case be dominated by the rural preservationists. The outcome is likely to be even stronger protection for those areas that are already protected (the Green Belt, rural areas) and more development in those areas that are already developing (towns such as Aylesbury). The spatialized rationality of planning may therefore further entrench the local alliances that have steadily congealed around the plan making process.

Chapter 6

Down to the District: Local Expressions of Development and Environment

Introduction

In the previous chapter we investigated in some detail the range of arguments that was brought to bear in the review of Buckinghamshire's Structure Plan. We showed that two broad networks or coalitions pushed the two rationalities of developmentalism and environmentalism. In this they were both aided by central government policy (for the developmentalists this policy assistance took the form of the housing numbers, for the environmentalists it came in the form of Green Belt and sustainable development regulations). Both these groups gained something from the Structure Plan: the housing numbers cascaded down to the county level virtually intact, while the distribution of this new housing largely accorded with the principles of protectionism (the bulk of it was set to go in the urban centres). In this chapter we follow this debate down to the district tier of planning policy. In the wake of the Structure Plan review, the arguments about the growth in housing numbers intensified within the reviews of the districts' local plans. In this chapter we follow the competition between planning's two prevailing rationalities down to this level and document the emergence of environmental concern in response to the local implications of the housing figures.

We focus on the district of Aylesbury Vale where, following the Structure Plan review, the Council set about formulating its own district-wide plan. Because the District lies just outside the Green Belt it has long been a target for development and, as we saw in the previous chapter, the town of Aylesbury, which had grown rapidly in recent years, was set to take a further round of new housing under the Structure Plan proposals. The problem of accommodating and distributing growth was always likely to be pronounced in the District. However, as we shall see, these problems came to the fore not in the town of Aylesbury but in the rural areas of the District.

We firstly outline the character of the Vale and the types of pressures the area is under. We then consider the District's proposals and show how policies cascaded down to this, the most local level in the planning hierarchy. In order to investigate how the proposals flow down to 'ground' level we examine the response to the plan in one local area, a large and rapidly expanding village. This was a place where arguments were likely to be particularly sharp not only because the village was identified as a site that might potentially take a substantial amount of new development, but also because its residents had already been engaged in a number of high profile campaigns (these included participation in a widespread campaign to prevent the building of a new motorway, an inter-regional campaign to oppose a rail-freight proposal, and an attempt to prevent the relocation of an industrial food-processing factory from Merseyside to the village). All these issues had succeeded in raising villagers' awareness of planning issues and development pressure. The village thus provides an ideal context in which to witness the emergence of an 'environmental' response to the planning for housing policies in the District. The material presented below was gathered as part of an ethnography conducted by one of the authors (Abram) during a substantial part of the District Plan review process (in 1997). This ethnographic work included a period of residence in the village, interviews with key activists, attendance at action group, village society, and planning authority meetings, and close attention to the contextual factors bearing upon the review process.

The district context and the local plan

Aylesbury Vale encompasses approximately half the spatial area of Buckinghamshire. The district lies broadly north of the Chilterns escarpment and extends from the town of Wendover in the south to Buckingham in the north, and also borders Milton Keynes. Aylesbury is the administrative centre of the district (and the county) and contains a population of over 58,000, one third of the district total. As well as Aylesbury there are over 100 smaller settlements in the Vale. Development pressure is at its most intense in the south (close to the Green Belt), particularly around Aylesbury itself. The north of the district still retains a rural feel, thanks mainly to the policy of channelling development into Aylesbury and Milton Keynes.

In general, the pace of social change in the district has been rapid. The small market town of Aylesbury was designated for expansion too in order to accommodate London 'over-spill' from the 1960s onwards, and expanded rapidly in the 1970s, with a great deal of new building in and around the historic core (see plate 6.1). The population continued to grow, increasing by 20% between 1980 and 2000, with Aylesbury receiving 8,000 new residents during the 1990s. The district has been subject to intense development pressure. The composition of the in-migrant population tallies with that outlined in the previous chapter: mostly middle class families with children, looking to find somewhere 'green and quiet' in this most prosperous and dynamic of regions. And once these families have become resident in the district they will tend to become concerned about threats to this 'quiet' and 'green' place. They will thus become involved in planning in order to protect local areas (see Murdoch and Marsden, 1994).

Plate 6.1 Aylesbury's market square, with the 1970s County Hall and 1980s shopping centre in the background (Photo S Abram 1997)

As already mentioned, planning policy in the district has traditionally emphasized rural protection and the concentration of development in Aylesbury town. A *Rural Areas Local Plan,* prepared in the early 1990s, for instance, stressed that policies would aim to 'protect and enhance the general environment and natural beauty of the countryside' (Aylesbury Vale District Council, 1991). It advocated the continued development of Aylesbury and the protection of smaller rural settlements. A rather strict division between urban and rural areas thus appears to have been established early on in the Vale.

Following the review of the Structure Plan the District Council began to put together its own district-wide plan. It started with the principles of sustainable development, interpreted along the lines used in the structure plan, and put together a set of proposals that again specified that Aylesbury should be the main developmental node. However, it soon became evident that there was a certain amount of disquiet within the Council itself, especially amongst political members, about the scale of new development that the District was expected to accommodate. Whilst growth rates had been agreed under a Conservative ruled District Council, a new Liberal-Democrat ruling group was less enthusiastic about urban expansion. Early on in the District Plan review process, members of the Council displayed a great deal of concern about the housing figures emerging from the Structure Plan. The new Council was faced with an intractable dilemma of making itself unpopular with constituents by finding locations for large amounts of new housing, or facing severe judicial problems if it chose to allocate smaller numbers of housing sites.

Their dilemma, in short, was how to concretize the abstract numerical allocations that had percolated through the regional and county plans. One Labour member articulated (in interview) ambivalence about the local plan dilemma of distributing housing allocated by the County Structure Plan:

> I always have a slight difficulty because I do agree with the sustainability argument that really, new houses should be directed towards the larger settlements, but I have a problem with that because I don't really believe that we need these houses in these numbers at all. The population isn't increasing at that sort of rate at all, and the projections that we're going to need all these houses, as you know, are based on the fact that marriages are splitting up and you're getting smaller families, so you're going to need that many more housing units than you did previously, and I just can't see how that squares with putting great big four, five and six bedroomed houses all round Aylesbury Vale. I just can't see it....yes of course, they're being sold, but it's not meeting the needs of the local area at all, you're just getting people who are commuting. And that doesn't help this sustainability aspect at all, to get people - really wealthy people moving in who, a lot of them, are commuting to London. If they're not, they're commuting to Milton Keynes (interview).

These sorts of sentiments were reflected at meetings of the Strategic Plans and Development committee (SPD), which occasionally became quite heated. At one meeting, councillors made comments such as:

> ...it would be tragic if this county is to become semi-suburban sprawl.

> ...we need to challenge some of the assumptions behind the figures.

> ...we don't want more people to live in this area in considerable numbers... Might we be so bold as to say that Aylesbury is full up?

At the end of this discussion it was proposed that Aylesbury Vale District tell the DETR that the district 'cannot cope' with further housing allocations. The planning officers present at the meeting counselled caution, one saying 'it would be unfortunate if one of SERPLAN's members says, we don't want (housing), look elsewhere'. The planning officer reminded the councillors that it was not good enough to say 'we can't take development'.

Through such comments, the planners acted both to bring the politicians back into line with the requirements of the legal planning process, but also reinforced the invulnerability of the housing figures that had emerged from the Structure Plan, pointing out that it was effectively 'too late' to challenge the figures at the local plan stage. Some councillors supported the planners, saying, for example, 'we must take ownership of the plan so another solution is not forced on us'. This line of argument featured in many arenas where the plans were discussed. The Council planners used it to defend themselves, and to discourage changes of course during the planning process. The argument proceeds from a view that if the plan is not 'robust', or if it does not meet the requirements stipulated in the County Structure Plan, it may be challenged at Public Enquiry or in the High Court by the County, developers, or other objectors. In that case, a ruling may be handed down that forces the district to adopt a policy they themselves do not favour. This was frequently referred to as having a plan 'forced upon us', or 'losing control of the plan'. The argument was often used by planners in order to 'discipline' the politicians and other participants in the district plan process.

However, the councillors were facing a further underlying dilemma. Should they act as a corporate unit to represent the whole district, and consider the best solution for the district as a complete entity, or should they prioritize the interests of their local constituents? Several councillors struggled with this problem, and opted for one or other option. One politician, a Liberal Democrat councillor for an Aylesbury suburb, explained this as follows:

> As a member of the district council, I recognize the requirements of the plan but as a councillor in [this ward], I say yes, okay, we want the plan, but we don't really want to have houses here, because it's going to spread [the ward] and take it, I would say, into Hertfordshire, because I really, ultimately want to keep a corridor between Hertfordshire and Buckinghamshire, and if I agree to let go that part I am gradually reducing that gap between the two counties (interview).

This councillor referred to his interest in planning as stemming from a 'baptism of fire' during the dispute over the building of an East-West motorway running through the county, where residents of villages along the route of the proposed six-lane dual carriageway rose up in protest (the proposal was eventually quashed in the Conservative government's transport review). However, he said, he was mainly interested in planning because 'if the people in (my ward) say they don't want any new houses, I have to take note of them'. This comment also illustrates the point at which resistance to new development began to emerge from within Aylesbury town. Once town residents began to appreciate that because of plan proposals their houses on the edges of the town would no longer be on the edge but would be incorporated into a much larger urban or suburban area, they began to voice protests.

Given the sheer scale of proposed development, with around 6-7,000 new dwellings on the horizon, much of the town looked set to be affected in some way by growth. The District Council expected the town's population to grow from around 58,000 to around 77,000 between 1997 and 2011, an increase of around 32,000 (Aylesbury Vale District Council, 1998 p.87). It was at this point, then, that the abstract figures finally began to take concrete shape as they were allocated to specific sites. However, it was also at precisely this point that they were seemingly invulnerable to challenge, having been solidified through the planning framework that had carried them from central government through the regional and county tiers.

It is instructive to consider the impact of this invulnerability from the perspective of councillors who may well appreciate strategic issues, yet still reject local solutions. The councillor referred to immediately above, a Liberal Democrat member of the Strategic Plans Committee, explains in some detail why it is that politicians find strategic planning difficult to reconcile with both local and personal interests:

> the process is, the county is part of the South East, the government say they want so many houses in the area, in Buckinghamshire. So looking round Buckinghamshire, people in the South Bucks area say, there's no point looking at us, we've got no space, it's all Green Belt, can't develop here, put it some other place....So Chiltern and South Bucks say we've got no space at all. But Buckinghamshire has to take something. So we look at Milton Keynes, but that is no longer part of Bucks. So Wycombe and Aylesbury end up taking a larger proportion...after a lot of debating and arguing, Aylesbury is expected to take some 7,000. That's where the fight starts. You then have a policy... so you start to look at sites that happen to fit in with the policy. Actually have a look and see accessibility, is it in open countryside, all sorts of things, we look at brownfield sites, which of course we would say look at brown field sites and put them there first...

This 'fight' in fact starts even before the Draft District Plan is published; before a word is written, different interests are pressurizing the planners and politicians, whether it is developers pressing for certain sites to be released, planners seeing opportunities in road developments for planning gain, or councillors looking for ways to steer development away from (or just occasionally towards) their wards. As the councillor goes on to elaborate, the heat is on the council's planning committee right from the start of the review process:

> There's this constant pressure. Developers want to develop where they see a bit of green. The local authority, the government, want houses because I understand they say that more single people are going to be wanting homes because they don't want to live with mummy and daddy any longer. That's the theory, so that they want some four million houses....As a councillor, the first plans will come forward and you will have an input....The officers have broad parameters of something to work with and so they come back again and you knock it around. Then you must not forget the political dimension. It might conflict with that, even though you have a broad scheme of things, for instance now there is a very great concern about the environment. So those of us who feel sufficiently strongly about whatever the issue is, it may be badgers or whatever, you start putting your input in as well, can't you

move it here, move it there? No, that doesn't fit with our local district plan. So you see all these different strategies, government strategy and local strategy, and political objectives, so all that comes together to form some sort of plan (interview).

This description of the generation of plans is a far cry from the more cut and dried policy process model where policies based on computed transport models, political priorities (such as sustainability) and strategic requirements are fitted together to form a coherent plan. At this, the most local level of planning, a host of competing pressures circulate around the plan.

The attitude of planners was more circumspect than that of many councillors. Indeed, some Aylesbury Vale planners seemed to see the new numbers as an opportunity to engage in 'real planning', that is, planning for development rather than planning that simply resists development. We quoted a planner in the District in the previous chapter who said 'I think South Bucks or Chiltern are planning to build 18 houses a year. I mean, that's not planning in my mind'. As this comment indicates, there was bewilderment at the low levels of housing in the south of the county and a feeling that the strong preservationist attitudes prevailing in the southern districts were preventing any form of 'real planning' taking place. In Aylesbury Vale the planners seemed to take some pride in the development plans that were being made, especially those related to the town of Aylesbury itself. They pointed to opportunities to put into practice new theories about 'urban villages', for example. As one planner commented to us during the Structure Plan review: 'There's a political will for Aylesbury Vale to kind of go places and to achieve more than it has done in the past and we've always accepted that encouraging growth into Aylesbury is a major part of that...'. Within the planning department it was simply assumed that Aylesbury would continue to grow, in part because at that time (during the Structure Plan review), as one planner put it, 'there's certainly no big body of opinion which is anti-development in the town' (interview).

The negotiations between the politicians and the planners (in the context of policy cascading down from above) shaped the early plan proposals. A planning model was commissioned from private consultants to indicate the optimum distribution of new housing between urban and rural areas, with particular emphasis placed on transport considerations. This model was used to create a division of the housing figures between urban and rural areas so that around 6,200 new houses would be allocated to Aylesbury and just over 800 would be apportioned to rural areas. The housing in Aylesbury was to be developed in accordance with the principles of sustainable development, and was to be linked to the provision of a transport infrastructure, based on an 'urban village' concept. These 'villages' would be arranged at poles on a new transport corridor. The district planners also employed sustainability criteria to select a number of key settlements for development in the rural areas. The rural housing was to be 'concentrated at a limited number of settlements which offer the best prospect for limiting the need to

travel and, through offering a choice of transport, minimize the use of the car'
(Aylesbury Vale District Council, 1998).

This process highlighted a number of sites which came to be seen as
potential solutions to the housing allocation problem. As another District planner
commented:

> What we're trying to go towards is an outcome which has been set gradually
> by an evolution from basic principles; you evolve those into a set of criteria
> and so forth and you end up pointing very clearly at one or two options and
> end up with one option, really. Having said this, it's a dilemma because it's
> not like a process where you could choose another three sites and it really
> doesn't make much difference to the process, you've honed in quite
> substantially by this time so it's very difficult to then move somewhere
> else... (interview).

This process meant effectively that councillors were offered little real choice of
location, since sites were identified according to a set of criteria predetermined by
the sustainability principles adopted by the planning committee. Sites emerged
from a rather abstract and technical process of selection. Planners drew up a chart
with a list of criteria (public transport, public services, land grade and use, for
example) against which they marked ticks and crosses for each of several similar
sized settlements in the district. Those which met the criteria were chosen for new
housing.

One of the settlements identified by the Council as more 'sustainable' was a
village called Haddenham, which had a population of approximately 5,000. It grew
rapidly between the 1960s and the 1990s, in part because it has a railway station
located on the main line between Birmingham and London and is on a bus route
running between Oxford and Aylesbury. As a transport node, the village has
figured strongly in debates around sustainability in the countryside and it looked set
to receive a fair amount of the housing to be allocated in the District. Under the
Draft District Local Plan, Haddenham was scheduled to accommodate a further 400
houses. We therefore examine the response to the plan proposals from the vantage
point of this village as there was a considerable amount of concern about the
potential impact of the plan's housing proposals on the local environment and
community.

Village debates

Haddenham is located in the south-western part of Aylesbury Vale and traces a
history back to at least Saxon times. There are two etymological theories
concerning the name of the village, one that it is a Saxon term translating as
'Hadders' hamlet, where Hadder is the name of a Saxon lord. The other theory
translates Hedenhem (as it is written in the Domesday Book) as 'home among the

heaths' (moorlands, or alternatively, heathens/pagans) which also suggests Saxon origins. It is distinguished by its local architecture of mud-and-straw construction, known as 'witchert', with walls tiled (earlier thatched) to prevent rain erosion, by its medieval stone church, and by its former renown for duck-raising. So-called 'Aylesbury ducks' were mainly raised in Haddenham, where ducklings were provided with their own thatched housing by the village pond, to protect them from spring showers. The trade died out post-WWII.

As we mentioned above, the village had grown rapidly during the latter half of the twentieth century, from a population of around 500 in the 1940s to around 5,000 in the 1990s. During the 1960s, a number of planners and architects moved in, at a time when property was much cheaper there than in Aylesbury town (a situation that later reversed). At the same time, new council housing was built around the east side of the village, close to pre- and post- World War Two council properties. Most of this housing has since been bought privately under the Conservatives 'Right-to-Buy' scheme, but much remains in the ownership of former council tenants. New estates of 'executive' housing have also been built mainly on the west side of the village, and many of those moving into these properties are professionals keen to live within a rural community. Property prices since the 1960s have rocketed, and by the late 1990s even one-bedroomed flats were selling for around £80,000. There has, therefore, been a relatively marked set of class distinctions within the village (although local opinions vary as to its significance). Nevertheless, despite the village's current size and multi-layered social networks, many residents cling fiercely to the notion that it is a 'real community', has a 'village feel' and should retain this as essential to its 'identity' and 'character'.

Development in the village

Haddenham has become a large village and many of its residents are keenly aware that any more large-scale development could easily give the settlement the character of a town, with increased traffic, more dispersed community facilities and greater anonymity. Thus, despite the lack of less-expensive and rented housing, many villagers are sensitive to any new development proposals and have shown themselves quite capable of fighting any new developments that threaten to undermine the environment and community life of the village. Thus, when the District Plan proposed that Haddenham take 400 extra houses there was an immediate community response.

The debates over planning in the village were normally filtered through the main amenity societies. The most long standing of these was the Haddenham Village Society (HVS), which was formed in the 1960s, in response to the rapid changes taking place in the community. The group was initiated by a small number of professional people (including architects and planners as well as business people) and was made up of both longstanding residents and others who had relatively recently moved into the village. The group coalesced around a general campaign for more architecturally and socially sensitive forms of planning in the village. The group gradually consolidated its role into raising awareness about planning and design issues in the village, drawing up a constitution that reflected these aims. They also consolidated their stance by participating in parish council activities. As one early member said:

> In the '71 local elections, the village society was well established, and three of us from the village society committee were elected onto the Parish Council. Thereby we instituted what still goes on today, a planning committee and a request to look at and comment (on planning applications) (interview).

This group gained widespread support in the village, and began to organize social events. The Village Society also organized a working party to renovate the village pond. The pond had been reduced to a muddy ditch when the clay ground seal had been pierced after mains water was introduced into the village. It was a group of Village Society members who set about turning it into a more picturesque duck pond, between the church and village green. This archetypally English scene, universally admired and attractive to new residents, is, prosaically, maintained through the use of a ball valve connected to the mains.

Plate 6.2   Haddenham 'Church End' (Photo S Abram 1997)

By the 1990s, the Society's planning sub-committee had gained considerable experience of planning issues and processes. They routinely examined both planning applications and planning policies, and responded to plan consultation exercises. In 1997, this committee included both a professional planner who worked for a neighbouring district council and a retired planning inspector.

The HVS planning group were well aware of what might appear in the District Plan since they had made representations to the previous Rural Areas Local Plan, and to the Structure Plan. The Village Society planning group therefore prepared a response to the District Council which stressed that they were unhappy about accepting any new housing allocation, but that in view of the strategic pressures, they recognized that some housing was inevitable. In keeping with their core interests, they stressed design and location considerations, and insisted that the actual number of new houses should be kept as low as possible. As one of their members explained, they adopted this position because, '...we've got to accept the cascade of figures coming down from above and I don't think you can change those at this stage' (interview). The group thus had a good understanding of the rationalities of planning and sought to find a way of accommodating (a limited amount of) development in ways that would be as sensitive as possible to the local environment.

This pragmatic stance was not shared by all villagers, however. When the Parish Council called a meeting to discuss the District Plan proposals, there was a large turnout. During the course of the meeting other villagers stood up and argued that neither the Parish Council nor the Village Society were properly 'defending' the village, and suggested that a further protest meeting should be held. The following week a well-attended meeting took place. It led to the birth of a new local society, which called itself the Haddenham Protection Society (HPS).

The HPS demarcated itself quite clearly from the HVS. The new society began enthusiastically to raise awareness in the village about the District Local Plan proposals: it organized a petition to the Council, undertook a fund-raising campaign, distributed window-posters declaring 'No to 400 houses in Haddenham', and organized parties of protesters to attend council meetings, at first carrying placards saying 'AVDC, keep off the grass please', and later wearing tee-shirts decorated with a picture of a scarecrow, and marked 'Save Our Habitat - Haddenham Village'.

The new group was tightly organized, partly because it was run as a network by a small group who chose not to set up a formal committee with chair and officers. Many of the central actors had been involved in a campaign against the siting of the new factory in the village, and therefore had experience of both running action groups and dealing with the District Council. Furthermore, the HPS central grouping also included a professional planner, who worked for a housing association in a nearby city. The new group emphasized that it would be oriented to the single issue of new housing in the local plan, thereby distinguishing themselves both from the general Village Society, and from the divisive issue of the factory which, in very general terms, had pitted local 'old villagers' in favour of increased employment against 'middle-class preservationists' concerned about the local environment and amenity. Arguments about housing growth cut across these former divides and generated new coalitions across village society. This cross-cutting was encouraged by the proposed site's location on a field adjacent to council and former council properties, thereby restricting the views of the council residents over open fields.

The new HPS rejected the Council's strategic arguments, and claimed that the village had seen enough growth, and that continued expansion would 'turn it into a town'. It was also very concerned that although the Council's revised plan only proposed housing on a small area of land adjacent to the Church End of the village, the site itself was large, and they were convinced that once opened to housing in the current Local Plan, the rest of the site would certainly figure in future plans, so that eventually at least a thousand houses may be built (see Figure 6.3 below). In order to avoid this potential scenario, the HPS declared that the aim was to reduce the village's allocation for housing to 'zero', or at least to windfall building only. Thanks to the Protection Society's consciousness-raising efforts, out of some 3,000 responses the Council received to their consultation on the draft plan, around 1800 were from Haddenham, all in opposition to the allocation of housing in the village as identified in the draft plan.

The HPS were also well prepared when it came to plan 'surgeries' held by the District planners in the village. These surgeries were held at all the locations proposed for development under the Draft Local Plan. They consisted of a small exhibition of the plan proposals with enlarged maps and diagrams of sites allocated for development. Planners took shifts to discuss the proposals with members of the public who came along to the meetings to see the plans. This strategy was adopted by the planners who wished to avoid confrontational public meetings, which they felt were aggressive and conflictual. Instead, they saw these surgeries as 'information-giving' occasions. They were not used, however, as 'information-gathering' exercises; people with objections were simply urged to send written comments to the planning committee. In fact, the planners used these meetings to defend the policies they felt most committed to, and directed members of the public to write in and complain about policies they felt politicians had adopted for tactical (electoral or party-political) reasons.

Unfortunately, when the planners came to Haddenham, they succeeded in alienating many villagers by announcing that their exhibition would be held at the 'Village Hall'. In fact, the room they used each time was known as the 'Mabel Parkinson' Room, and its entrance was on the opposite side of the building to the entrance to the Village Hall. Some villagers went to the village hall and, finding the doors locked, assumed the exhibition had been cancelled, whilst others happened to walk past the Mabel Parkinson room on their way to the Village Hall entrance, and, seeing the exhibition was on, came in to point out that the Hall and the room were not the same. Although this happened each time the Council planners used the Mabel Parkinson room, their neglect of this detail reinforced villagers' views of the planners as both ignorant of the village and arrogant in their dismissal of local knowledge. As more than one villager remarked, 'who are they to claim they know better, they don't even know their way round the village!'.

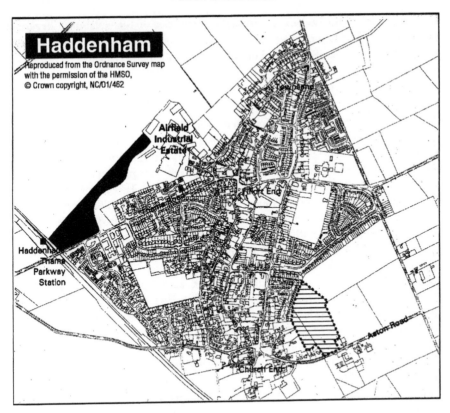

Figure 6.1   Housing sites in Haddenham

Such views were further exacerbated by the use of abstract checklists of criteria in choosing sites suitable for development (as outlined above). Local residents claimed that the criteria were quite arbitrary, and that they had been wrongly used in Haddenham. The site proposed for development was adjacent to the village's conservation area, was at the furthest point in the village from the railway station, represented a breach of the village boundaries identified in 1971 (although only in a village plan rather than any statutory document), and would encourage commuters to drive either out of the village or through it. When planners admitted at a later surgery in the village that they had abandoned plans to open a new railway station north of Aylesbury at a place where they were proposing to build 3,000 new houses, Haddenham residents were furious. Planners explained that their transport advisers recommended that most people would walk no further than 800 metres to a railway station, and that the new 'urban village' would include only a few hundred people within that distance, making any new station economically unfeasible. When Haddenham residents pointed out that the site proposed in Haddenham was nearly 2 kilometres from the railway station, therefore making any arguments for sustainability of new building equally invalid, planners were at a loss to justify their arguments. Rationalities of 'sustainability' began, at this point, to look weak, and to appear to cover intentions to direct development towards Haddenham village based on other, unspecified criteria.

Turning up the political heat

As we mentioned above, the planners had used their sustainability criteria to direct development towards the larger of the rural settlements, including Haddenham, Winslow and Buckingham. According to these criteria, Haddenham would provide an ideal location for housing development, and the planners had built this assumption into their overall proposals for the District. This had generally been seen as acceptable within the Council. Indeed, the local councillor for Haddenham had been in favour of new housing development. When the district had negotiated its development levels with the county, the District Council had been under the control of Conservative councillors and was generally in favour of continued growth, particularly in Aylesbury town (the Conservative Party locally was, as we mention above, mainly rural-based). However, as the plan review unfolded, the Council came under Liberal Democrat control, and this led to a much more defensive attitude towards housing growth. Moreover, a General Election was due some months later (in May 1997); thus the battle over the local plan began to take on much wider political significance.

The increasingly charged politics of planning began to have an impact on the proposals. In particular, the Haddenham councillor was standing as Liberal Democrat parliamentary candidate for the Aylesbury area. He was also a leading member of the Strategic Planning and Development Committee, and in this forum he now seemed determined to use the plan to mount opposition to the Tory government which, he argued, was sending large housing allocations down the line towards Aylesbury Vale, and, in turn, to Haddenham. This councillor found himself in a politically powerful position, commanding support from fellow Liberal Democrat councillors in making the seemingly popular move of reducing the allocation of housing for Haddenham. Suggesting that to opt for 'zero housing' in Haddenham would offer 'no protection' from predatory developers (along the lines of 'losing control of the plan, outlined above), and taking into account the similar plight of Winslow, a small town which had also been allocated 350 houses, the councillor suggested towards the end of a meeting of the Forward Planning Committee late one evening in March 1997 that the allocations for both villages should be reduced to 150 houses each, with the remaining 400 houses being distributed among a further 'tier' of smaller villages throughout the Vale. He was supported by the Conservative councillors in Winslow, thereby ensuring that the proposal was passed by the committee. A similar fate met the plans for Aylesbury town, so that new development was re-routed away from Liberal Democrat constituencies. In the process the sustainability criteria that had been used to allocate development in the first instance were completely undermined.

This 'coup' was regarded with horror by the planners and the Chair of the Strategic Planning and Development Committee (also a Lib-Dem), not least because it would require a restructuring of the whole housing policy for the Vale, and would lead to an extra round of consultations in all the villages now identified as suitable for development. Having spent several years honing the strategy, the planners now saw it being displaced in favour of a more nakedly political scheme. As one planner put it:

> There's a conflict of ideologies, between those that seek to provide minimal impact on local residents which is the politicians... and those who seek to provide best sites in overall sustainability terms, and so on, which is the planning professionals. And the two things don't necessarily match (interview).

Not all the politicians were in favour of the new housing allocations, however. One Liberal Democrat member and Chair of the Planning committee who had worked closely with the planners, was also disappointed at the behaviour of his colleagues. In interview he emphasized the political nature of their calculations:

> The political context is that the (Liberal Democrat) AVDC-controlled council can't be seen to be putting forward proposals to build houses on sites which are not very popular with the local community...Secondly you've got to recognize that the county council elections are taking place...and a lot of the areas that were intended to get some of those Aylesbury homes in the next 15 years are up for county council elections, and therefore the Lib Dems who are fighting those seats, either as incumbents or whatever, again don't want to risk unpopularity in the context of county council elections....add to that the extra pressures put on the county with the General Elections coming up, meant that the Lib Dem group, I don't think performed as it should have done in sticking to its principles and its guns in the strategy....They were not prepared to stand up and say "it may not be popular, it may not win us votes in the county and general elections, but we support the strategy of the local plan" (interview).

Having worked closely with the planners for many months to reach an agreed strategy, a strategy that incorporated the sustainable principles laid out in planning guidance and in the Structure Plan, this councillor and a small group of his colleagues were dismayed to see the strategy crumble in the face of more overtly party political and electoral considerations. The planner responsible for the rural areas within the plan commented, 'it's difficult not to conclude that we're going to have to try and get back to something a little bit more sensible at some stage' (interview).

Local divisions

The net effect of the proposal to distribute development more widely around the rural areas of the Vale was to arouse a further tier of opposition to the Council from residents in many more villages. Moreover, this move was not popular amongst the no-growth campaigners in Haddenham, because it did not rule out growth altogether. The new distribution left an allocation of 150 houses on more than one site, described by one Village Society member as 'pimples which will turn into great boils'. The Council was thus left facing a new, fortified alliance of many rural villages waging a campaign against the council's revised planning strategy of dissipated growth.

The policy shift was, however, advantageous for the HPS in that it enabled the group to counter the charge of 'NIMBYism' (which some councillors were using in order to dismiss their objections to housing growth) by forging a Vale-wide coalition with all affected or potentially affected villages. The HPS committee had already realized that they could not afford to be Haddenham-centred in their campaign, since any accusation of 'NIMBYism' would undermine their credibility. They therefore seized the opportunity to broaden out the campaign. Among those wishing to join a broader anti-development network included the residents' association of a village on the other side of and much closer to Aylesbury which was concerned that the expansion of the town would effectively reach out and incorporate the village into the boundaries of the town. 'Urban concentration' of development thus began to look more like 'rural development'. This was also true of much of the rest of the development situated 'in' Aylesbury which was, effectively, expanding the town onto greenfield sites outside the existing town. However, much of the expansion had been directed towards the north of the town, where there were few settlements and, consequently, no residents to defend the open countryside. Although the local archaeological society made objections about the plan's proposal to build extremely close to an important iron-age site, in the face of massive housing development (of several thousand houses on this site alone), the council seemed prepared to risk the disapproval of archaeologists in order to achieve development on this scale.

In shifting their attention from the problems of Haddenham itself, the HPS also began to develop more sophisticated proposals. Originally the aim was simply 'zero growth'. However, as they became more knowledgeable about planning so they realized that they needed to give their arguments more professional credibility. They therefore began to frame their representations using sustainability criteria. However, these criteria were less concerned with transport (the Council's approach) than with the re-use of already developed, brownfield sites (another priority identified by central government). The group, therefore, proposed an alternative site at a recently closed military site, whose neighbouring village school and shop were closing for lack of local population, while part of the site was already being reused for light industry. However, this proposal met with planners' responses that the site, despite being 'brownfield' was 'unsustainable', being located between the towns of Aylesbury and Buckingham but not being on a current frequent bus route (as Haddenham was). The inability of planners to plan to potential future bus routes, or to plan to make new routes viable, was highly frustrating and difficult to countenance by the village groups. For planners, it seemed, the brownfield site was not as sustainable in transport terms as the Haddenham site, while for Haddenham villagers it offered a much more appropriate, socially sustainable site where housing re-development would be welcomed.

As the HPS developed a more planning-focused approach, some of their arguments began to resemble the Village Society's early pragmatic proposals. One of the District planners remarked on this change, saying: 'If you look at Haddenham Protection Society, early HPS, a lot of it was irrelevant but gradually it evolved into planning-speak. They've taken on the jargon and to a degree they've taken on the thinking' (interview). This shift in approach may have been because the group had begun to use professional advice. Rather than appoint an expensive barrister to represent them at public enquiry, the group sought out a solicitor who could advise them on a campaign approach and help them make effective written representations. The solicitor began to persuade them of the limits to capabilities of planning at the local level, indicating that a complete refusal of all development would be a weak strategy. In his view, a more carefully prepared design statement for a small 'contribution' to rural development would carry more weight than anything that resembled a 'NIMBY' argument. The group thus had to mobilize arguments that had wider relevance than the village itself. They therefore began to build alliances with other villages in the hope that they could present a united front to the forthcoming public enquiry.

Despite increasing similarities between the discursive repertoires used by the HVS and the HPS, and their overlapping memberships, there was no reconciliation between the leading members of the two societies. In fact, there was considerable unease amongst HPS leaders that one of their fellow leaders also sat on the HVS committee, and had reported to the HVS about HPS meetings (and we, as researchers, were sworn to secrecy before being allowed to observe HVS meetings). The increasing friction between the two groups turned into a crisis for the Village Society. A group of Protection Society members, who were also Village Society members, used the Village Society's own constitution to petition the Village Society Committee for a general meeting to debate its response to the District Local Plan. The membership of the Village Society began for the first time to question the planning group's position, a challenge that was seemingly hurtful to the group's members. One remarked, with dismay as well as resignation:

> I'm very hurt, well not hurt that's a ridiculous thing to say, but it astounds me, this pressure trying to impose the views on a committee that decided after a lot of months and years of discussion that this is the line to take. Now, we have this group that's saying well, we're going to make you change that view (interview).

He also felt that despite a large membership, the Protection Society had only sectional interests:

> Any action I have taken within the Village Society has always tried to consider the village as a whole, not just the members of the Village Society, whereas these people do seem to be more concerned with getting signatures and saying we're acting for these people, and I don't think that is quite the thing. Because I think if you had a fair open discussion of most of the village, it would be a very, very close thing (interview).

At the meeting of the Village Society, members present voted overwhelmingly to change the Society's response to be more in accord with the HPS approach. As a result a liaison committee was set up between the two societies. In addition, the Parish Council was asked to consider all village reactions to the DLP rather than responding independently as they had done previously.

The Parish Council's response to the Plan had at first been neutral, then, later, came to resemble that of the Village Society (after taking advice from the Village Society's planning committee). However, the Chair of the Parish Council was also the local County Councillor (Conservative), a local landowner. Other members of the Parish Council included both 'old villagers', concerned about the lack of affordable housing and critical of people they viewed as 'NIMBYs', incomers, and residents concerned about the conservation of the village. The Parish Councillors had not, however, been elected since not enough people had been persuaded to stand for election. Members had, therefore, been co-opted. So, whilst the Parish Council actually incorporated a good range of village representatives, it had little political legitimacy and was not seen by many as particularly representative of the village as a whole (although it had, by this time, begun to represent a number of different perspectives from within the village, if not in any proportional way).

As the HPS and the Village Society geared themselves up for the public enquiry into the Plan, there were a number of important developments that changed the course of the campaign. Of particular significance, given the new arguments being mobilized by the HPS, was the emergence in the summer of 1997 of two new brownfield sites (a redundant airforce base and a disused brickworks) which appeared to offer scope for as many as 800 houses. The planners were not entirely happy about one of these sites because it was ill-served by public transport. However, it did go a long way to solving the growing problem of where to put Aylesbury Vale's rural housing allocation and had the potential to dissipate the pressure building up over the arguments about the possible distribution of housing in many small villages.

When these new sites appeared, the Council removed consideration of the 'third tier' of villages from the plan. As a result, the coalition that Haddenham had forged with the other villages was undermined and the village was to a great extent left again to fend for itself. However, rather than removing Haddenham from the allocations, the Council chose to retain 100 houses in the village. The Haddenham councillors, who by this time had declared themselves against further housing provision in principle, made an 'impassioned plea' to share the 100 houses between Winslow and Haddenham. Now, however, the other members did not support them. The Haddenham councillor had not performed well enough at the General Election to gain the Aylesbury North seat. He had also lost the support of many of his colleagues through what they saw as his unwillingness to take a 'fair share' of development in his ward. All 100 houses were, therefore, allocated to the village on a single site.

In effect, this decision threw the HPS into the position of taking their objections forward to public enquiry, a strategy they had hoped to avoid. It left them with a straight fight against the Council for which they began to prepare. The Deposit Draft of the plan (AVDC 1998) specified that 'it is appropriate to locate a limited amount of further housing at Haddenham' and identified an appropriate site for the 100 houses. It also explained that Haddenham could be made more sustainable if further employment was attracted to the village:

> The village could build upon its attractiveness to investors as an employment location. This would help meet some of the District's strategic employment needs and provide jobs in a key rural location that can help to reduce commuting to major towns from rural areas.

According to the plan policies, Haddenham looked likely continue to grow, albeit at a rather slower rate than the original policies proposed. That is, the council actively planned that Haddenham should continue to grow. However, the campaign over policies for Haddenham had left bitterness and argument in its wake both within the village and across the District as a whole.

Conclusion

As we have seen, at this level of planning a whole variety of local factors come into play when confronting the housing allocations: sustainable development and other PPG policies, local political arrangements, the influence of environmental campaigns, stages in the electoral cycle, relations between community groups, historical patterns of development, and so on. As the housing numbers bear down upon particular places, so they put pressure upon this 'heady' mixture of local and contextual factors. The upshot can be a great deal of debate and dispute within the development plan review.

In the review, all these factors became 'jumbled up' together. In the case study presented here, planners and politicians debated 'sustainable strategies', agreeing sets of principles on which to allocate the large number of houses they were obliged to accept from the Structure Plan. These principles were, however, undermined by political manoeuvring. This indicates the extent to which local politics influence planning policies at the local level. When we descend down to the village, we find even more dispute and political deliberation. What the outcome will be in terms of housing land allocations is as much determined by politics as policies. Local discretion is thus channelled into convoluted and acrimonious debate about the location of pre-ordained development levels.

As the review process unfolded, the politics became intertwined with discontent around levels of development. The campaign against housing development could not challenge the figures coming down from above, thus everything became focused on distribution - where should the houses go? Haddenham villagers began by taking a pragmatic stance on this issue and, realizing that the District had to take a set number of new houses, accepted that some new development in the village was inevitable. The campaign initially focused on low numbers and quality housing. The pragmatic stance, which stemmed from the planning expertise of village representatives, was not to the liking of many villagers. It was thus displaced by demands that the village campaign for 'zero growth'. However, it was noticeable that 'zero growth' soon ceded once again to pragmatism. This shift reflects the immutability of the figures and shows how a realistic assessment of local planning implies that a certain level of development is inevitable.

In the process a good deal of resentment was stirred up both within the village and within the Council. As one planning officer put it:

Haddenham has been acrimonious. The Haddenham members decided to fight to the death, and they ended up losing. Therefore they didn't say "okay, we don't like it but we'll take our share and work with other councillors on this", and the thing has ended acrimoniously... (interview).

In an area such as Aylesbury Vale, where pressure for development is intense, such resentment and acrimony is inevitable and it will doubtless re-emerge during the next round of plan-making. Next time, however, the stakes will be that little bit higher and the pressure that little bit more intense.

The case study presented here therefore indicates that political dispute envelopes housing figures all the way down to the very local level. It also shows that this dispute comes to be bound into a whole variety of contextual factors. What the outcome will be on the ground is determined by the interaction between these contextual factors and the rationalities of planning policy cascading down from above. The latest rationality is 'sustainable development', a notion that can and has been interpreted in many differing ways, and with various policy consequences. In Buckinghamshire, it ensured that high levels of new houses were steered into Aylesbury and Milton Keynes. The villages, rural areas and Green Belt were afforded some protection. The upshot of this is that these latter places become the most valued environments in the county. Following counterubanization, they also become home to groups of people who are determined to retain their value. Thus 'sustainable development' policy reinforces a rather strict divide between urban and rural. It is interesting to speculate how long this will hold in such a dynamic regional context.

However, 'sustainable development' comes in other guises and has other effects. As the case study of Aylesbury Vale showed, it can result in a set of rather abstract and technical criteria being used to allocate sites for development. These criteria may not accord with local residents' understandings of these sites or the places (as opposed to spaces) where the sites are found. Again, this raises problems for participation and may lead to a lack of understanding at the local level both about both the reason for the amount of development and the distribution of that development.

The planners believed sustainable development criteria could be used in order to engage in creative planning (new urban villages surrounding Aylesbury). For them, sustainability was an important means of providing a 'rational' response to the continuing growth pressures bearing upon the District. Thus, sustainable development in Aylesbury Vale could provide a means of accommodating significant amounts of new housing while protecting the most precious environmental resources (the Green Belt and rural areas). Some local councillors, however, saw things differently. They sought to overturn the 'sustainable' allocations. Their concerns were more immediate: would they get re-elected if the local plan allocated houses in their wards?

This latter development might be thought to mark out the 'limits of rationality' i.e. however much the rationalities we have described lead to an 'ordering' of planning practice, local contextual circumstances will always impinge on their working. While we have some sympathy with this view, we believe there is a recursive relationship between rationality and context. At the local level we see how the rationalities work to affect practice and planning outcome (the housing numbers still carry development, the sustainable development discourse still organizes distribution), but at the same time we see in much more detail the sets of relations that surround these modes of ordering so that the tensions between 'rational' organization and local imperative come to the fore. In this recursive relationship we discern the tiny shifts that alter the operation of ordering modes, the shifts that mean no rationality unfolds in quite the same way twice, the shifts that tell us no matter how much we attempt to plan the 'world', the 'world' will always find its own way to escape our plans. As planning becomes spatialized, as it becomes more deeply immersed in territorial contexts, so we should expect these 'shifts' to become commonplace. Thus, when the argument is made that planning should engage more wholeheartedly with space and environment, we should recognize that planning itself may have to change if it is to undertake this role; it may have to scale down its ambitions in order to fully engage with the range of political, social, and environmental circumstances that will surround it.

Yet, the case studies presented in the previous two chapters also show that the plans still work: they still serve to define development trajectories and to adjudicate on communities and environments. But they could work better: they could work with more of these local contextual circumstances, rather than against them. They could also carry more people with them, especially those most affected by the development that the plans facilitate. If plans are to become spatialized they will have to function in this fashion. We assess how they might do this in the final chapter.

Chapter 7

Towards a New Rationality of Planning?

Introduction

There is an ever-present danger in writing of planning policy that the 'rationalities' of planning will be reduced to the status of a political power game (Flyvberg, 1998). In this scenario, normative modes of spatial ordering become nothing more than the expression of 'vested interests' or 'base political calculation'. Alternatively, politics and power can be written out of the script altogether so that planning becomes abstracted from the everyday contexts of practice and takes on a purely idealized form (Tewdwr-Jones and Allmendinger, 1998). Rationality, in this second scenario, becomes the expression of 'reason' and unfolds in ways that seem detached from any likely political influence.

In the previous chapters of this book we have attempted to mark out a 'middle way' between these two views of planning policy. We have sought to argue that the rationalities of planning are both powerful discursive repertoires *and* reflections of the contexts in which they unfold. Thus, the rationality of development can prescribe appropriate modes of planning to meet the goal of economic growth and can stipulate that the main role of planning is to facilitate the play of market forces. The rationality of environment can focus attention on the intrinsic properties of natural environments and the need to maintain the integrity of these environments. In both cases, quite legitimate forms of reasoning can be employed to justify the goals of planning policy. However, these forms of reasoning do not take place in a vacuum: they are carried by political actors and networks and are rationalized in contexts where power relations remain at play. Although, as Foucault has emphasized, any firm distinction between power and rationality is hard to maintain, not least because rationalities help to hold political alliances together while such alliances help to stabilize rationalities, we should not assume that rationality *is* power and, conversely, that power *is* rationality. Rather, there is a recursive relationship between these two aspects of planning policy: rationality and powerful networks co-construct each other (see Murdoch *et al.*, 1999, on planning and Latour, 1987, for a general discussion).

We have distinguished the two most common rationalities underpinning policy here and have sought to show how they recursively interact with a variety of governmental contexts. We have traced their co-existence in planning policy over

133

time (Chapter 2), outlined how they come to be situated within the various tiers of government (Chapter 3), and shown how they configure a particular policy sector (Chapter 4). We have also investigated how they become immersed in particular local spaces and how they work within local policy review processes (chapters 5 and 6).

In so doing, we have often set these rationalities against each other, as though they were mutually exclusive. In the main, however, planning proceeds under the assumption that the two can be combined (this is perhaps why the profession has so eagerly embraced the principle of 'sustainable development'). Yet, in attempting to combine these competing and, at times, conflicting rationalities, planning policy has often found it hard to maintain a balanced approach. It has tended to emphasize one or other at various points in time, so that policy has become either more 'market-led', thereby downplaying social and environmental considerations, or has sought to preserve given environments, thereby curtailing the scope for development. While many planners remain optimistic that planning can 'rationally' adjudicate between development and environment, this 'rational adjudication' has often seemed elusive.

We have argued strongly here that these rationalities of planning must be set within their institutional contexts (see also Vigar *et al.*, 2000). In Chapter 3 we examined the extent to which each tier - national, regional, and local - plays a part in the formulation and implementation of policy. We saw that central government takes the main responsibility for policy formulation, notably through the issuing of the PPG notes that set the overall parameters for local level decision making. The guidance notes are wide-ranging and cover all the main sectors encompassed by planning. However, they are also flexible and allow some local interpretation and discretion. They pass, in the main, directly from the national tier down to the local tier where decisions about development are made. In this way, PPGs shape both development plans and development-control decisions but remain sensitive to the status of local plans. We proposed that the balance between central direction and local discretion shapes the definition of planning's goals and thus the prevailing rationality of policy.

PPGs seem to define a limited form of 'multi-level governance' within planning. Local planning authorities inherit policy guidelines and then (theoretically, at least) tailor these to the particular economic, social and environmental contexts in which they operate. Thus, PPGs arguably allow uniformity in planning policy to be combined with local specificities. While a balance between uniformity and local discretion may sometimes be hard to achieve, there is no doubt that PPGs have been implemented with the intention of achieving some mixture of the two.

The relative powers of centre and locale in planning policy vary, however, according to the sector under discussion. We noted in Chapter 4 that the policy for local economic development is constructed in a relatively non-hierarchical fashion while the policy of planning for housing works within a 'top-down' framework that has the central state prescribing in fairly precise terms how policy should be implemented and interpreted by local planning authorities. The main reason for the existence of a hierarchy in this sector is the perceived requirement to ensure that sufficient houses are built to meet anticipated demand. This requirement necessarily overrides local aspirations around given levels of (housing) development. Those actors hoping to influence the interpretation and implementation of policy at the local level thus find their efforts frustrated by the immutability of centrally formulated policy prescriptions. In this case, local participation makes no impact on the overall levels of development and comes to be focused upon their spatial distribution. And as we have seen in the previous two chapters, the system ensures that the two rationalities of planning come into conflict at the lowest levels of the planning hierarchy: housing has to be accommodated in local land allocations but the distribution of these land allocations is often resisted by local participants.

'Governance' and 'governmentality' in planning for housing

In seeking to understand the planning for housing policy sector we have drawn loosely on two theoretical repertoires. Firstly, the tiered nature of policy making in planning demands attention to the literature on 'governance' and the way that 'hierarchical forms of articulating public policies and firm boundaries between public and private action are being displaced by more fluid and horizontal relationships' (Healey, 1998 pp.3-4). In this view, a genuinely 'multi-level' planning system seems to be coming into view. Healey goes on to say,

> the development plan-making provisions of the planning system potentially provide an already existing arena where people can come together and work out strategic ideas and build sufficient consensus to pursue new initiatives in place making and place maintaining (1998 p.4).

Clearly, many participants in the planning for housing process expect the system to operate in this fashion and this is one reason why they bother to get involved in the first place. Yet, Vigar *et al.* (2000 p.289) argue that the UK planning system still has some way to go in this regard. They say:

> The challenge for the British planning system in the first decade of the new century is to shift the inherited institutional structure from the trajectory into which it has been channelled…into a richer, more place-focused, more future-oriented and more localized form.

According to these authors, a hierarchical governmental framework is still very much in evidence but what is needed is a much more territorially sensitive form of planning in which forms of 'collaboration' determine policy outcomes. In this regard, they seek to promote a spatial rationality.

Theories of 'governance', then, only have so much to offer the analysis of planning policy. We have therefore drawn, secondly, on ideas associated with 'governmentality', a concept that is derived from Foucault (1991), and which emphasizes how agents located in a variety of (governmental) domains have their actions aligned by the 'rationalities' and 'technologies' of policy. While the components of governmentality come in a variety of forms, they all work on the 'conduct of conduct' and attempt to ensure that agencies not directly controlled by the state nevertheless abide by behavioural norms (see Gordon, 1991). In so doing, governmentalities draw 'lines of force' across the governmental terrain (Rose, 1999), thereby linking the institutions of government and a variety of civil society actors within sets of co-ordinated relations. These relations are orchestrated by given rationalities and materialized in governmental technologies, such as statistics.

This is precisely how the policy has traditionally operated in planning for housing. In Chapter 4 we outlined how the policy is encoded within forecasts of housing demand and the means by which these forecasts then 'cascade' down through the tiers of government (see also Murdoch *et al.*, 2000; Vigar *et al.*, 2000). In chapters 5 and 6, we described how, as a consequence of this 'cascade' local plan participants quickly find themselves forced to accept given levels of housing development. Having found that these numbers themselves are impervious to anything but the most technical arguments, local participants can only address their distribution. However, even here, the process of housing allocation is being systematized in line with the rationality of sustainable development. While, in the main, the local expression of this rationality accords with participants' aspirations (especially when 'brownfield land' was the distribution mechanism), it also acts to reinforce a perception that participation has little impact on the technicalities inherent in local planning decisions.

Despite the fact that the discourse of sustainable development accords with local aspirations (especially on the part of those actors representing the 'counterurbanizers'), chapters 5 and 6 indicate that many of the local participants' spatial concerns are inadequately dealt with in the plan making processes. The rich repertoires of 'localism' that they bring to bear on planning policy sit uneasily with the technical justifications that tend to dominate plan review processes. This is perhaps why local participants are so often characterized as 'self-interested' and 'parochial' in their concerns. Reflecting on the outcomes of three structure plan review processes, Vigar *et al.* (2000 p.274) say:

> Activists were typically cast, in the rhetoric of national government and the language of business lobbies, as "NIMBYs", fettering enterprise and holding up development. They were less often presented as voices from civil society concerned to give environmental and social dimensions more weight, or with viewpoints which integrate policy agendas from the perspectives of everyday life. Nor were they (sic) appreciated as legitimate claims by citizens seeking to have some influence over what happens in the places they live in and care about.

This comment is echoed by Warburton (2000 p.149) who says 'NIMBY...has become a term of abuse, rather than a recognition that people care about the places where they live'.

As the previous two chapters have shown, local plan participants are often characterized in this fashion. And yet, it is equally clear that these people care passionately about the places in which they live (often for the communal and environmental reasons outlined in Chapter 2). However, in seeking to assert their feelings for 'place' within the plan reviews, they struggle to find an appropriate language in which to make their representations effective. While they quickly find that they need to engage in 'planning speak', they also find that this technical discourse cannot easily encompass their real concerns. There is, therefore, a seeming need to make plans more accommodating of local views and the spatial circumstances in which these views are embedded.

As a result of the growing disquiet about the 'mis-match' between the rhetoric of inclusive governmental processes at the local level (e.g. DETR 1998a) and the realities of participation, a shift in the policy framework does appear to be emerging at the present time. The immediate causes of the shift stem from the 1995 housing projections which seemed to threaten a further 'cascade' of numbers down to local plan reviews. This forecast acted as a catalyst and mobilized the influential political constituency that had been gathering around protectionist planning policies. In seeking to diminish the political pressure bearing upon the planning for housing sector, the Labour government has introduced a number of significant policy modifications (discussed briefly in Chapter 4). As a consequence, a 'spatialized' rationality has begun to displace the rationality of 'development' from the centre of the planning for housing policy area. This shift, as we have argued extensively above, is raising the profile of spatial complexity, notably through a concern with 'sustainable regional development'. We therefore need to ask if the new spatial rationality will better incorporate the varied concerns of local participants and whether a more 'balanced' approach to planning for housing is likely to emerge.

Towards a new rationality of planning for housing?

Following the heated debate around the 4.4 million forecast, the Labour Government began to shift the policy in the direction proposed by environmentalists and others concerned at the role of the projections. The new approach was first spelled out in *Planning for the Communities of the Future* in 1998 and in the most recent version of PPG 11 (DETR, 1999b), which contextualizes the projections at the regional level and appears to raise the profile of regional planning. Both policy documents seek to ensure that a regional 'ownership' of the figures is developed so that the system can be characterized as responsive to regional demands and sensibilities (*ibid.*). The regional planning conferences are now to take more responsibility in deciding how housing numbers can be met and, in so doing, should adopt measures that lessen their impact on undeveloped (greenfield) land (for instance, regional planning fora must now look at the allocation of previously developed sites, the scope for a 'sequential' and 'phased' approach, and should have greater awareness of regional development capabilities, and so on - see DETR, 1999b).

Once the figures reach the region they will no longer hover over complex socio-spatial contexts: they will become immersed in them. For instance, it is suggested that regional planning fora should undertake sustainability appraisals which 'should appraise the potential impacts of different strategic options in order to integrate sustainable development objectives in the formulation of policies' (DETR, 1999b p.15). As part of the appraisals, not only are the environmental consequences of differing housing figures to be assessed, the social consequences must also be considered. The figures will thus be situated within a large amount of social and environmental data specific to given regional areas.

The new approach was strengthened by PPG 3 (*Housing*) published in 2000 (DETR, 2000b). According to this document, the Government remains committed to the developmental rationale of ensuring that 'everyone should have the opportunity of a decent home' (DETR, 2000b p. 1). However, it also states that in formulating their housing policies, regional planning bodies should assess 'both the need for housing and the capacity of the area to accommodate it' (*ibid.*). Thus, the guidance note seeks to align the two rationalities of development and environment (here within the same sentence). In fact, the simultaneous assertion of both runs through the whole document. On the one hand, it is emphasized that regional planning authorities must take the latest household projections into account but these must be balanced against the 'capacity' of urban areas to accommodate more homes and the environmental implications of given levels of housing provision (*ibid.*). The main emphasis in PPG 3 is on the concentration of development in urban areas and on the re-use of previously developed land so as to protect the countryside. As the Planning Minister Nick Raynsford put it:

> PPG 3...sets the tone for the switch we want to see in plans away from greenfield development and towards the reuse of previously developed land. No longer will the only, and simple, answer be to dig up another field to meet the increasing need for homes (quoted in CPRE, 2001 p.5).

Thus, PPG 3 argues that regional planning authorities can: *plan* for a given number of homes; *monitor* the effects of development and the continuing demand for housing; and seek to *manage* development so that it is concentrated in urban locations. In short, sustainable housing development has come to mean development at higher densities on brownfield land.

The importance of this policy development can be measured by this comment from the CPRE (2001 p.2), one of the sternest critics of the planning for housing system:

The publication of (PPG 3) marked a true watershed in the government's approach to housing development. By abandoning predict-and-provide planning for housing, introducing a presumption in favour of using urban land before greenfield sites and stressing the importance of higher density and better designed development it signalled a genuine desire to put an end to sprawl. Effectively implemented the new policies could both defuse growing public controversy over new development in the countryside and help in the renaissance of our towns and cities.

As we saw in Chapter 4, this policy is already beginning to have a significant impact. In the review of RPG in the south east, a regional capability study was undertaken which showed that the region could only meet its housing requirements if it breached environmental constraints. This capability study thus gave rise to a scenario in which the two rationalities of development and environment came into conflict with one another (Murdoch, 2000). Subsequent government attempts to refine the policy (e.g. by choosing housing numbers midway between the region's total and the national forecast, and claiming that the plan, monitor and manage system mean more houses can be provided on less land) have not diminished the central issue: once the figures are immersed in complex regional environments they inevitably lose their immutability and become subject to a whole host of competing considerations. One consequence may be that they fail to carry all those households that will require houses into present day decision making (Holmans, 2001).

Some of the likely considerations to come to the fore in these new institutions of spatial planning were considered in Chapter 6. Here we saw politicians, planners and local residents wrestling with the implications of the housing figures at the local level. Despite the constrained nature of the debates in Aylesbury Vale District, we can see that economic, social, political and environmental considerations all became jumbled up together. Without a firm regulatory context provided by central government, we can also see that in this instance decisions could have been reached using any of these criteria. This finding illustrates the importance of Rydin's (1999 p.960) comment that,

> planning decisions are a form of collective decision making. This is not the same as decision making by the local community since that represents only a subset of the broader social collectivity. Planning purely by the local community can be justified only if no other claims on that local space are recognized... Some may claim that proper information and persuasion will result in local communities taking the "right" decision in each case but this may not necessarily be so. It is at least worth considering whether there is not a role for the state taking decisions even against the wishes expressed through public participation.

If this is true for the local level then how much more true must it be for the region? Not only is the region now able to formulate its own policies, but it is expected to do so by including as many regional stakeholders as possible in the review process. All these stakeholders should attempt to balance the various considerations that need to be taken into account before reaching decisions on the desired levels and distributions of development. However, notwithstanding the use of 'sustainability appraisals' and other such technical procedures, it is far from clear how they should prioritize the multiple considerations that will jostle for supremacy in given regional contexts. This has led some authors to worry that economic considerations will dominate the regional planing process (e.g. Baker *et al.*, 1999), while others to propose that it will be environmental constraints that will be in the ascendant (Lock, 2000).

The danger thus arises that the differing regional development trajectories will largely conform to the balance of political forces within the regions themselves. For instance, in the South East protectionist policies will very likely generate support from many local planning authorities, environmentalists and countryside participants (such as those we studied in Aylesbury Vale), while almost certainly alienating the RDA and urban economic interests. In the urban North, it is possible that environmental protection will take second place to demands for jobs and economic stability, rendering the environmental discourse largely ineffective. As yet the government has not explained whether this regional autonomy, and the differing development trajectories that will inevitably ensue, is to be welcomed. Neither has it made clear how the conflicting aims and objectives of the various regional actors are to be reconciled: it clearly hopes that through processes of 'iteration' and 'joint working' some kind of natural synergy between the agencies of planning and development will emerge.

In making this reform, the government appears keen to encourage planning at the regional tier to adopt 'collaborative' ways of working (see Healey, 1997; 1998), in which various stakeholders come to together to achieve some kind of consensus around policy. It seems to believe that the incorporation of a range of stakeholders in the new regional plan review processes will encourage the development of such collaborative processes in ways that will resolve some of the most intractable policy issues facing planners at this governmental tier (we should note, however, that Healey, 1998, expresses some scepticism about the potential for *genuine* collaboration within the current administrative matrix). If regional planning *can* play this role then it may resolve many of the disputes that are currently raging at the local level for it will permit genuine participation further up the governmental hierarchy. Yet it is worth asking whether the types of disputes that run through planning for housing are capable of resolution at the regional tier. In particular, is a consensus around sustainable development policy likely within regional planning?

Forging a 'sustainable' planning policy

In their analysis of the relationship between development and environment in the context of minerals planning, Cowell and Owens discern problems in 'developing defensible justifications for any particular environmental constraint or capacity' (1997 p. 29). Where conflict emerges between developmental and environmental actors they note that 'projections of "national need" for (minerals) are afforded an "objective" status that takes precedence over "subjective" judgements of environmental value, even when the latter have some claims to be rigorous and defensible' (*ibid.*). This characterization of minerals planning could be applied equally to housing, as projections of demand have traditionally overridden local support for environmental protection. However, in the last section we described how this situation is changing so that considerations of environmental capacity and capability now have a higher status in the policy process. As we outlined in Chapter 4, SERPLAN used a capability study to justify its refusal to meet the housing projections in the south east, with the Secretary of State for the Environment giving some endorsement to this strategy in his 'plan, monitor and manage' approach. He argues the new approach will deprive the housing projections of their long-term power. Thus, the situation described by Cowell and Owens for minerals - where 'the interpretation of sustainability in terms of environmental constraints flies in the face of prevailing ideologies, which dictate that predicted demands should be met' (Cowell and Owens, 1997 p.28) - would no longer seem to apply in the housing sphere. The need for increased environmental protection now seems to have higher status and capability and capacity approaches are coming to the fore (with all the implications that they hold for places like Aylesbury and Milton Keynes).

According to Owens (1997 p. 294), 'attempts to interpret sustainability "on the ground" are almost always contentious'. This is especially the case, as Owens (1994 p.451) points out, when considerations of environmental capacity are involved, for these raise the issue of 'critical natural capital' and the need for its protection. Scope for conflict emerges, in part, because concepts such as 'capacity' and 'natural capital' challenge the assumptions of development: 'It is not difficult to see in the concept of environmental capabilities, especially when defined on the basis of non-utilitarian ethics, a fundamental challenge to a market-led political economy...' (Owens, 1994 p.451). We should therefore expect that 'the identification of critical natural capital will be strongly contested' (Owens, 1994 p.450). In other words, immersing development in robust regional environments will not be easy especially if environmental entities are given an 'immutable' stature. As we have seen, this immutability was previously the prerogative of development trends. In the face of environmental immutability, development proves more tractable.

Objections to the use of the 'natural capital' and 'environmental capability' concepts in development plans will undoubtedly be led by those business interests that we saw operating so effectively in the Buckinghamshire Structure Plan review (in Chapter 5). They will seek to challenge regional planning's environmental protectionism, especially when this undercuts nationally-derived development projections (as is currently the situation in the south east). It will thus be interesting to see how developers operate in the new regional planning fora. Following our discussion in Chapter 5, it is clear that of particular concern to developers will be the status of the central government forecasts. The government now says that the projections are only one of the many criteria to be taken into account at the regional level when identifying future levels of housing development. The house builders are already warning that this may lead to housing shortages and to the many social ills that inevitably follow (in this they have many supporters, notably the TCPA - see Holmans, 2001). If a number of regional planning authorities refuse to abide by national projections then central government may be forced to step in to impose national numbers on reluctant regions. Not only will this fragment any regional consensus, but it will put central government back in the political firing line.

A continuing role for central government at the regional level may also be required if regional planning bodies are 'captured' by overly protectionist environmental interests. As Rydin (1998 p.753) warns,

> the concept of environmental capacity can be used to support existing tendencies towards NIMBYism within land use planning... [Moreover] the danger is that environmental capacity does not just become a new concept which can support NIMBYism; it becomes a form of NIMBYist planning....

The worry here is that the overt protectionism of local environments that is so often seen at the local level will be repeated at the regional tier of planning. Again, this will undercut any likely consensus as a number of stakeholders will simply follow their own, narrowly defined interests. The challenge is therefore to encourage such actors to think strategically. How this will be achieved is far from clear. Local planning attracts a great deal of attention precisely because it is 'local'. Whether the same level of interest can be generated in a higher spatial scale remains in doubt. However, it seems certain that the involvement of local amenity groups in ways that enable them to think strategically will require innovations in democratic practice. The government, as yet, appears to have given this issue little thought, in part because it remains ambivalent about engineering democracy at this governmental tier. As Hull (2000 p.775) says:

> The key test for regional actors, as they interact in these new arenas of governance, will be their ability to reach consensus on interconnected issues which expand out from their own geographical or sectoral concerns.

If the region does become more genuinely 'collaborative' (in Healey's, 1998, terms), then we would also expect to see changes at the local level. Traditionally, debates at both the county and district tiers have been dominated by arguments about the allocation of given development levels (especially in the housing sector). Developers line up along one side of the debate (sometimes literally, as in the EiP, Chapter 5), environmentalists and local residents on the other. At present, the arguments of the participants are steered by policy and dominated by the projections. So, as we saw in Chapter 6, in debating the implications of development, local actors find the overall numbers to be immutable; they are, therefore, forced to concentrate on distribution. This feature of local participation reinforces the developmentalism of the developers and imposes a kind of NIMBYist interpretation on the arguments of local residents and environmentalists. In effect, none of the groups are permitted to think strategically and broadly; all are forced to simply defend their own core interests.

And yet, as we saw in Chapter 6, when local groups do become involved in planning processes they very quickly learn how to adopt the concerns of planning systems; they pick up the discourse of planning and its associated ways of thinking. In this fashion, they also learn to think strategically. As we saw in the case of Haddenham, groups can enter the process with very narrow aims ('zero growth') but they then acquire much more sophisticated perspectives on the planning process and the types of choices that need to be made (prioritize brownfield development through renovation strategies). At present, there is little reward for adopting such a 'sophisticated' approach, as the current system continually forces local groups to think locally, with 'local' defined in very narrow ('NIMBYist') terms. Thus, innovations in policy should not just seek to engineer collaboration at the regional level, but should encourage such processes locally.

Such encouragement will require genuine participation at the local level rather than the process of rather stunted consultation that planning uses at present. This will require further democratic innovation in local government (see Stewart, 1993; Pratchett, 1999) so that a genuine dialogue between planners and participants is forthcoming. Only in this fashion will a solution to the interminable problem of development versus environment in the context of planning for housing be found. It might also allow for an enhanced perception of the 'public interest' in planning for housing so that all those engaging in the process come to agree on the basic aims of policy (such an agreement is clearly lacking at the present time) (see Ross, 1991). The public interest is as yet unclear but it must surely specify that those people requiring access to a home should have their needs met in ways that do not undermine critical natural capital. If this interest were clearly articulated then it might be possible to put the processes in place to ensure that policy delivers the required goals, not only environmental protection but housing that meets genuine social need.

Clearly, the Labour government's ambitions for local democracy are aiming in this direction. The recent power of 'well-being', and the call for the formulation of 'community strategy' indicate attempts to move local democracy in the direction of holistic, participatory policy-making (DETR, 2001, 2000e,). The latter insists that local authorities 'produce a community strategy for promoting and improving the economic, social and environmental well-being of their communities' (2000e, para 16) in order to contribute towards sustainable development. Furthermore, it states clearly that these three elements must be considered in an integrated way, since, 'a community strategy that covers only one of those elements will not suffice. Nor will the duty be met by producing three separate strands dealing with economic, social or environmental issues in isolation' (*ibid.*). The same paper pushes for greatly increased public involvement in the making of community strategies, in the form of a 'broad "community planning partnership"' (*ibid.*) which includes 'key partners operating in the area that the strategy is to cover (*ibid.*, para 26). This clear commitment to community-based and community-focused policy making overlaps with other governmental initiatives, and appears to form a core for all the Labour administration's innovations in local government practice.

However, there are a number of difficulties with this, as yet new, policy direction. The papers give, for example, very little guidance as to how local authorities are to achieve policy in situations that will undoubtedly bring together conflicting actors and groups. As we have indicated above, these conflicts will not merely consist of different interest groups, but will also have to face widely different perspectives on locality and strategy, and significantly varied epistemologies of development held by different actors (see Abram, 1999 for a consideration of these issues). Given the difficulties we have described here in debating limited planning issues between selected actors, it is not at all clear from government guidance how a broader and more ambitious consensual policy making could, in fact, be enacted.

The only nod towards these potential hurdles comes in a comment that 'a number of well-tried methods are now available to enable communities (whether neighbourhood based or communities of interest) to articulate their needs – such as "planning for real", village appraisals, community profiles and listening surveys.' (DETR, 2000e, para 91). Whilst these methods are well-tried, we would continue to urge that their limitations are also known, although they are poorly documented. Whilst the government guidance has attempted to avoid being too prescriptive, we would argue that as a result it offers little in the way of real innovation in addressing these fundamental limitations to the very ambitious form of collaborative, holistic and comprehensive planning it urges.

Furthermore, the new local government proposals show little evidence of considering the interaction between powers of community well-being, community strategies and the existing land-use planning system. Whilst section 2(3) of the 'Power to Promote or Improve Economic, Social or Environmental Well-Being' (DETR, 2001, para 24) states that 'in exercising the well-being power, a local authority must have regard to its community strategy', it does not state explicitly how it should regard the District Local or Strategic plans covering the same area. It is difficult to see how a frequently-updated Community Strategy, which may have as its geographical area a part or the whole of a District, could be co-ordinated with a land-use plan that covers up to 20 years into the future, and may take five years to review (as the Aylesbury Vale District Local Plan already has done). Evidence is already beginning to emerge from Scotland (e.g. Scottish Office, 1998, 2001) that these two systems are incompatible, and that a solution to their incompatibility lies with the overhaul of the land-use planning system, in line with the new community-plan system. So far, however, it is not clear whether the DETR would countenance a whole-scale renovation of the land-use planning system for England that would remove the clashing rationalities we have described above, to the extent that land-use reviews could be subsumed into flexible, locally-determined community strategies. Such a scheme, resembling Scandinavian planning styles, would radically alter the system we have described above, disrupting the hierarchies of multi-level governance and reducing land-use planning to a technical sub-division of community planning. It is hard to imagine, given the attitudes of participants in current planning disputes we have described, that house builders, for example, would easily relinquish the sort of predictability that long-term land-use plans currently offer, even though they are labour-intensive (and expensive in legal fees) to achieve. Nor would a less secure planning framework necessarily benefit home-owners or environmentalists who would also lose the potential 'protection' that planning zones can offer (although this protection has been shown to be very weak particularly in the light of transport infrastructure development disputes in the late 1990s). This scenario, however, is one possible 'logical conclusion' of the direction in which planning has been steered at the beginning of the 21st century.

From prescription to discretion

In the preceding pages we have described planning from the theoretical vantage points of 'governance' and 'governmentality'. We have argued that the planning policy structure is hierarchically organized with some limited scope for local discretion. However, this discretion varies between sectors, and in our case study sector - housing - we have described a policy framework that is strongly configured by governmental technologies - notably the housing forecasts. These forecasts serve to implement a developmental rationality that aims to ensure sufficient housing land is made available by local planning authorities to meet projected demand.

The prescriptive nature of this system has come in for great criticism, notably from environmental and amenity groups who see the figures cascading down the governmental hierarchy, determining levels of development as they go (evidence presented in preceding chapters indicates that this interpretation is broadly correct). The critics have effectively argued for the introduction of a 'governance' system in which some policy-making autonomy is devolved to the regional and local tiers. It is expected that regional and local planning authorities (especially if they are instructed to work closely with 'stakeholders' and encouraged to conduct 'sustainability appraisals), will immerse the figures in a range of contextual considerations, thereby diminishing their power over the governmental framework. Initial evidence supports this view: the south east regional planning authority has taken up the autonomy it has apparently been granted by the Labour government to produce a new 'sustainable development policy' for the south east. In so doing it has utilized a new technology - the capability study - in order to show that environmental constraints in the region rule out meeting the housing forecasts in full. Thus, immersion of the forecasts in regional complexity (or 'sustainable development') significantly changes their status.

We have proposed that another rationality of planning has, as a consequence, come to the fore. We have given this rationality a number of different names - 'spatial planning', 'territorial planning', and 'planning for sustainable development'. These various terms refer to a 'mode of ordering' that highlights the importance of spatial complexity: it points to the mixture of economic, social and environmental entities, and stipulates that all these must be taken into account by planning policy; no longer can policy float above spatial areas in an abstract way, descending merely to prescribe certain courses of developmental action. Rather, policy must emerge from *within* these complex (regional and local) contexts, and must be tailored to their precise characteristics. In other words, planning looks set to be submerged within 'hybrid' spaces in which multiple elements have to be considered concurrently.

As a result, planners will be encouraged to treat the diverse elements 'symmetrically' (see Latour, 1993, for an explanation of these terms) so that clearly reasoned justifications are provided for prioritizing one class of entities (e.g. environmental) over others (e.g. social). If these reasoned justifications emerge from transparent processes of genuinely 'collaborative' planning (as envisaged by Healey, 1998) then the rationality of 'sustainable development' may facilitate a balanced approach in the new regional planning arenas so that the complex interdependencies between differing entities are seen as of paramount importance. If, however, reasoned justifications do not emerge in this way, regional planning decisions may simply reflect the balance of political forces in given regional territories. In this case, the rationality of 'sustainable development' may well go the way of the rationality of 'development': it will be regarded as an unwelcome imposition, one that ultimately works to 'discipline' decision making activities throughout the planning for housing framework.

Conclusion

The account we have provided here should be read as an attempt to capture the shift from one rationality to another: 'planning for development' ruled in the planning for housing policy; now 'sustainable development' is to the fore. One interpretation of this shift might propose that this is just part of the usual 'to-ing and fro-ing' between development and environment that has long been characteristic of planning policy. The latest shift is to environment, but there is nothing necessarily new in this; the pendulum will eventually swing back to development. We propose an alternative interpretation, one that has guided our analysis throughout this book: at a fundamental level the balance between the two rationalities has changed, perhaps irrevocably. In regions such as the south east, economic growth proceeds so fast, and the environmental consequences of this growth reach so far, that protection of natural assets and the quality of life become the overriding concern. When we link this concern to the social formation of the outer south east, and to those groups that are most active in the planning system, we can see that it comprises a significant political force in planing policy (especially as policy change in the south east directly feeds into national policy). This force will not go away: in fact, the faster economic growth proceeds, the stronger it will become (as we have argued above, some recognition of this has been evident in planning policy over the last ten years and broadly connects the policies of Chris Patten to those of John Prescott). In order to meet the demands that will be placed upon it by this political constituency, planning will need to more wholeheartedly embrace 'planning for sustainable development', 'spatial planning' or 'territorial planning'.

Yet, this is not the whole story, for the shift away from 'planning for development' comes with its own consequences attached. Some, such as the constraints on participation, are perhaps best left behind; but others cannot be so easily dismissed. The planning for housing case study shows that, while protection, preservation and environmental constraint are 'goods' that come easily to the spatial rationality, development to meet the needs of those 'in need' does not. For instance, the south east housing settlement may very well result in housing shortages in the region just as the continuing development of Aylesbury may very well diminish the quality of life for people in the town. These concerns are not so readily voiced within the environmental discourse. If, as we suggest, the new rationality of spatial planning implies the *symmetrical* treatment of many differing values and needs in the new participatory frameworks, then these aspects and entities need to be given a much higher profile. It will be interesting to see whether this higher profile can be achieved within the new dominant rationality or whether it will require a further shift in planning's dominant 'mode of ordering', towards an approach that more successfully blends the national-to-local alliances of political power with a form of reasoning that clearly enshrines the 'public interest' in land use regulation and planning for housing.

Bibliography

Abram, S. (1999) 'Planning the Public', *Journal of Planning Education and Research*. 19: 351-357.

Abram, S., Murdoch, J. and Marsden, T. (1996), 'The Social Construction of "Middle England": the Politics of Participation in Forward Planning', *Journal of Rural Studies*, Vol. 12, pp. 353-364.

Abram, S., Murdoch J. and Marsden T. (1998), 'Planning by Numbers: migration and statistical governance', in P. Boyle and K. Halfacree (eds), *Migration into Rural Areas: Theories and Issues*, Chichester: Wiley, pp. 236-251.

Alden, J. and Offord, C. (1996), 'Regional Planning Policy', in M. Tewdwr-Jones (ed), *British Planning Policy in Transition*, UCL Press, London.

Allen, J., Massey, D. and Cochrane, A. (1998), *Rethinking the Region*, Routledge, London.

Allinson, J. (1999), 'The 4.4 Million Households: Do We Really Need Them Anyway?', *Planning Practice and Research*, Vol. 14, pp. 107-113.

Allmendinger, P. and Tewdwr-Jones, M. (1997), 'Post-Thatcherite Urban Planning: a Major Change?', *International Journal of Urban and Regional Research*, Vol. 21, pp. 100-116.

Allmendinger, P. and Tewdwr-Jones, M. (2000), 'New Labour, New Planning? The Trajectory of Planning in Blair's Britain', *Urban Studies*, Vol. 37, pp. 1379-1402.

Atkins, D., Champion, T., Coombes, M., Dorling, D. and Woodward, R. (1996), *Urban Trends in England*, Department of the Environment, London.

Atkinson, R. and Moon, G. (1994), *Urban Policy in Britain: the City, the State and the Market*, Macmillan, London.

Aylesbury Vale District Council (1991), *Rural Areas Local Plan*, Aylesbury Vale District Council, Aylesbury.

Aylesbury Vale District Council (1998), *District Local Plan: Consultation Draft*, Aylesbury Vale District Council, Aylesbury.

Baker, M. (1998), 'Planning for the English Regions: a Review of the Secretary of State's Regional Planning Guidance', *Planning, Practice and Research*, Vol. 13, pp. 159-169.

Baker, M., Deas, I. and Wong, C. (1999), 'Obscure Ritual or Administrative Luxury? Integrating Strategic Planning and Regional Development', *Planning and Design*, Vol. 26, pp. 763-782.

Barry, A., Osbourne, T. and Rose, N. (eds) (1996), *Foucault and Political Reason: Liberalism, Neo-Liberalism and Rationalities of Government*, UCL Press, London.

Bate, R. (1999), 'The Household Projections: a Wolf in Sheep's Clothing', in D. Dorling and S. Simpson (eds), *Statistics in Society: the Arithmetic of Politics*, Arnold, London, pp. 369-375.

Bell, M.M. (1994), *Childerley*, University of Chicago Press, London.

Bingham, M. (1997), 'The Changing Content of Local Plans: Some Issues and Evidence From the "Plan-led" System', Discussion Paper 79, Dept. of Land Economy, University of Cambridge.

Bishop, J. (2000), 'The Withered Laurels?', *Town and Country Planning*, Vol. 69, pp. 150-151.

Blowers, A. and Evans, B. (eds) (1997), *Town Planning into the 21st Century*, Routledge, London.

Bogdanor, V. (2001), 'England May Get its Turn', *Guardian*, 23rd April. p. 15.

Boyle, P. and Halfacree, K. (eds) (1998), *Migration Into Rural Areas*, Wiley, London.

Bramley, G. (1998), *Memorandum to Select Committee on Environment, Transport and the Regions Tenth Report: Housing*, The Stationary Office, London.

Bramley, G. and Watkins, C. (1996), *Circular Projections*, Council for the Protection of Rural England, London.

Breheny, M. (1999), 'People, Households and Houses: the Basis of the "Great Housing Debate" in England', *Town Planning Review*, Vol. 70, pp. 275-293.

Breheny, M. and Hall, P. (1996), *The People: Where Will They Go?*, Town and Country Planning Association, London.

Brindley, T., Rydin, Y. and Stoker, G. (1989), *Remaking Planning: the Politics of Urban Change in the Thatcher Years*, Unwin Hyman, London.

Bruton, M. (1980), 'Public Participation, Local Planning and Conflicts of Interest', *Policy and Politics*, Vol. 4, pp. 423-442.

Buckingham-Hatfield, S. and Percy, S. (eds) (1999), *Constructing Local Environmental Agendas: People, Places and Participation*, Routledge, London.

Buckinghamshire County Council (1994a), *County Structure Plan: Consultation Draft*, Buckinghamshire County Council, Aylesbury.

Buckinghamshire County Council (1994b), *County Structure Plan: Deposit Draft*, Buckinghamshire County Council, Aylesbury.

Chairs of the RDAs (1999), *Memorandum to House of Commons Select Committee on Environment, Transport and the Regions*, Stationary Office, London.

Champion, T. (1994), 'Population Change and Migration in Britain Since 1981: Evidence for Continuing Deconcentration', *Environment and Planning A*, Vol. 26, pp. 1501-1520.

Champion, T. (1996), *Migration Between Metropolitan and Non-metropolitan Areas in Britain: Report for the ESRC*, Economic and Social Research Council, Swindon.

Champion, T. and Townsend, A. (1990), *Contemporary Britain: a Geographical Perspective*, Edward Arnold, Sevenoaks.

Charlesworth, J. and Cochrane, A. (1994), 'Tales of the Suburbs: the Local Politics of Growth in the South East of England, *Urban Studies*, Vol. 31, pp. 1723-1738.

Cloke, P. and Little, J. (1990), *The Rural State*, Arnold, London.

Coleman, D. and Salt, J. (1992), *The British Population: Patterns, Trends and Processes*, Oxford University Press, Oxford.

Council for the Protection of Rural England (1995), *Memorandum to Select Committee on the Environment Second Report: Housing Need*, HMSO, London.

Council for the Protection of Rural England (1998), *Memorandum to Select Committee on Environment, Transport and the Regions Tenth Report: Housing*, The Stationary Office, London.

Council for the Protection of Rural England (1999), *South East Housing*, Council for the Protection of Rural England, London.

Council for the Protection of Rural England (2001), *Sprawl Patrol: 1ˢᵗ Year Report*, Council for the Protection of Rural England, London.

Counsell, D. (1998), 'Sustainable Development and Structure Plans in England and Wales: a Review of Current Practice', *Journal of Environmental Planning and Management*, Vol. 41, pp. 177-194.

Counsell, D. (1999), 'Sustainable Development and Structure Plans in England and Wales: Operationalizing the Themes and Principles', *Journal of Environmental Planning and Management*, Vol. 42, pp. 45-61.

Cowell, R. and Murdoch, J. (1999), 'Land Use and the Limits to (Regional) Governance: Some Lessons from Planning for Housing and Minerals in England', *International Journal of Urban and Regional Research*, Vol. 23, pp. 654-669.

Cowell, R. and Owens, S. (1997), 'Sustainability: the New Challenge', in A. Blowers and B. Evans (eds), *Town Planning into the 21ˢᵗ Century*, Routledge, London, pp. 15-31.

Crookston, M. (1998), 'Regional Policy and the Great Housing Debate', *Town and Country Planning*, July, pp. 213-215.

Cross, D. (1990), *Counterurbanization in England and Wales*, Avebury, Aldershot.

Cullingworth, B. (1997a), 'Fifty Years of the 1947 Act', *Town and Country Planning*, May, pp. 128-131.

Cullingworth, B. (1997b), 'British Land Use Planning: a Failure to Cope with Change?', *Urban Studies*, Vol. 5, pp. 930-952.

Cullingworth, B. and Nadin, V. (1997), *Town and Country Planning in the UK* [12ᵗʰ edition], Routledge, London.

Dean, M. (1999), *Governmentality*, Sage, London.

Department of the Environment (1992), *Planning Policy Guidance Note 3: Housing*, Department of the Environment, London.

Department of the Environment (1992/1997), *Planning Policy Guidance Note 1: General Policy and Principles*, Department of the Environment, London.

Department of the Environment (1995), *Memorandum to Select Committee on the Environment Second Report: Housing Need*, HMSO, London.

Department of the Environment (1996), *Household Growth: Where Shall We Live?*, Cmd. 3471, HMSO, London.

Department of Environment, Transport and the Regions (1998a), *Modernizing Planning*, Department of Environment, Transport and the Regions, London.

Department of Environment, Transport and the Regions (1998b), *Planning for the Communities of the Future*, Department of Environment, Transport and the Regions, London.

Department of Environment, Transport and the Regions (1998c), *Modern Local Government: In Touch With the People*, Department of Environment, Transport and the Regions, London.

Department of Environment, Transport and the Regions (1999a), *Projections of Households in England to 2021*, Department of Environment, Transport and the Regions, London.

Department of Environment, Transport and the Regions (1999b), *Planning Policy Guidance Note 11: Regional Planning: Public Consultation Draft*, Department of Environment, Transport and the Regions, London.

Department of Environment, Transport and the Regions (1999c), *Planning Policy Guidance Note 12: Development Plans*, Department of Environment, Transport and the Regions, London.

Department of Environment, Transport and the Regions (2000a), Press Notice 164, Department of Environment, Transport and the Regions, London.

Department of Environment, Transport and the Regions (2000b), *Planning Policy Guidance Note 3: Housing*, Department of Environment, Transport and the Regions, London.

Department of Environment, Transport and the Regions (2000c), *Guidance on Preparing Regional Sustainable Development Frameworks*, Department of Environment, Transport and the Regions, London.

Department of Environment, Transport and the Regions (2000d), *Draft Regional Planning Guidance for the South East: Proposed Changes*, Department of Environment, Transport and the Region, London.

Department of Environment, Transport and the Regions (2000e), *Preparing Community Strategies: Draft Guidance to Local Authorities*, Department of Environment, Transport and the Region, London.

Department of Environment, Transport and the Regions (2001), *Power to Promote or Improve Economic, Social or Environmental Well-Being*, Department of Environment, Transport and the Region, London.

Dorling, D. (1995), *A New Social Atlas of Britain*, Wiley, London.

Elson, M., Steenberg, C. and Downing, L. (1998), *Rural Development and Land Use Policies*, Rural Development Commission, Salisbury.

Fielding, A. (1990), 'Counterurbanization: Threat or Blessing?', in D. Pinder, *Western Europe: Challenge and Change*, Belhaven, London, pp. 226-239.

Fielding, A. (1992), 'Migration and Social Mobility: South East England as an Escalator Region', *Regional Studies*, Vol. 26, pp. 1-15.

Fielding, A. (1998), 'Counterurbanization and Social Class', in P. Boyle and K. Halfacree (eds) (1998), *Migration into Rural Areas*, Wiley, London, pp. 41-59.

Flyvberg, B. (1998), *Rationality and Power*, University of Chicago Press, London.

Forrest, R. (1987), 'Spatial mobility, tenure mobility, and emerging social divisions in the UK housing market', *Environment and Planning A*, 19, pp. 1611-1630.

Foucault, M. (1991), 'Governmentality', in G. Burchell, C. Gordon, and P. Miller (eds), *The Foucault Effect*, Harvester Wheatsheaf, London, pp. 51-66.

Gatenby, I. and Williams, C. (1992), 'Section 54A: The Legal and Practical Implications', *Journal of Planning and Environmental Law*, Vol. 42, pp. 107-116.

Gatenby, I. and Williams, C. (1996), 'Interpreting Planning Law', in M. Tewdwr-Jones (ed), *British Planning Policy in Transition*, UCL Press, London, pp. 135-153.

Goodwin, M. (1998), 'The Governance of Rural Areas: Some Emerging Research Issues and Agendas', *Journal of Rural Studies*, Vol. 14, pp. 5-12.

Gordon, C. (1991), 'Governmental Rationality: An Introduction', in G. Burchell, C. Gordon and P. Miller (eds), *The Foucault Effect*, Harvester Wheatsheaf, London, pp. 1-55.

Government Office for the South East (2000), *Housing Technical Note*, Government Office for the South East, Guildford.

Government Office for the South East (2001), *Regional Planning Guidance for the South East (RPG 9)*, Government Office for the South East, Guildford.

Graham, S. and Healey, P. (1999), 'Relational Concepts of Space and Place: Issues for Planning Theory and Practice', *European Planning Studies*, Vol. 7, pp. 623-646.

Hacking, I. (1981), *Representing and Intervening*, Cambridge University Press, Cambridge.

Halfacree, K. (1994), 'The Importance of 'the Rural' in the Constitution of Counterubanization: Evidence from England in the 1980s, *Sociologia Ruralis*, Vol. 34, pp. 164-189.

Hall, P., Thomas, R., Gracey, H. and Drewett, R. (1973), *The Containment of Urban England*, Allen and Unwin, London.

Halliday, I. and Coombes, M. (1995), 'In Search of Counterurbanization: Some Evidence from Devon on the Relationship Between Patterns of Migration and Motivation', *Journal of Rural Studies*, Vol. 11, pp. 433-446.

Healey, P. (1983), *Local Plans in British Land Use Planning*, Pergamon, Oxford.

Healey, P. (1997), *Collaborative Planning: Shaping Places in Fragmented Societies*, Macmillan, London.

Healey, P. (1998), 'Collaborative Planning in a Stakeholder Society', *Town Planning Review*, Vol. 69, pp. 1-21.

Healey, P. (1999), 'Sites, Jobs and Portfolios: Economic Development Discourses in the Planning System', *Urban Studies*, Vol. 36, pp. 27-42.

Healey, P., McNamara, P., Elson, M. and Doak, J. (1988), *Land Use Planning and the Mediation of Urban Change*, Cambridge University Press, Cambridge.

Healey, P. and Shaw, T. (1994), 'Changing Meanings of "Environment" in the British Planning System', *Transactions of the Institute of British Geographers*, Vol. 19, pp. 425-448.

Herbert-Young, N. (1995), 'Reflections on Section 54A and "Plan-led" Decision Making', *Journal of Planning and Environmental Law*, Vol. 45, pp. 292-305.

Hoggart, K. (1997), 'The Middle Classes in Rural England 1971-1991', *Journal of Rural Studies*, Vol. 6, pp. 245-257.

Holmans, A. (2001), *Housing Demand and Need in England 1990-2016*, Town and Country Planning Association, London.

House Builders Federation (1994), 'Submission to Buckinghamshire Structure Plan Review', House Builders Federation, Cambridge.

House Builders Federation (1998), *Memorandum to Select Committee on Environment, Transport and the Regions Tenth Report: Housing*, HMSO, London.

House of Commons (1995), *Select Committee on the Environment Second Report: Housing Need*, HMSO, London.

House of Commons (1998), *Select Committee on Environment, Transport and the Regions Tenth Report: Housing*, The Stationary Office, London.

Hull, A. (1997), 'Restructuring the Debate on Allocating Land for Housing Growth', *Housing Studies*, Vol. 12, pp. 367-382.

Hull, A. (2000), 'Modernizing Democracy: Constructing a Radical Reform of the Planning System?', *European Planning Studies*, Vol. 8, pp. 767-782.

Hull, A. and Vigar, G. (1998), 'The Changing Role of the Development Plan in Managing Spatial Change', *Government and Policy*, Vol. 16, pp. 379-394.

Jackson, S. (1998), *Britain's Population: Demographic Issues in Contemporary Society*, Routledge, London.

Jessop, B. (1998), 'The Future of the National State: Erosion or Reorganization?', Mimeo, Dept. of Sociology, University of Lancaster.

John, P. (1998), *Analyzing Public Policy*, Pindar, London.

John, P. and Whitehead, A. (1997), 'The Renaissance of English Regionalism in the 1990s', *Policy and Politics*, Vol. 25, pp. 7-17.

Johnston (1998), 'Stranger Reshaping New Surroundings: an Interview with Richard Caborn', *Planning*, 1st May, pp. 18-20.

Kallinikos, J. (1996), *Technology and Society: Interdisciplinary Studies in Formal Organization*, Accedo Press, London.

Land Use Consultants (1995), *The Planning Policy Guidance System in England and Wales*, Department of the Environment, London.

Latour, B. (1987), *Science in Action*, Open University Press, Milton Keynes.

Latour, B. (1993), *We Have Never Been Modern*, Harvester Wheatsheaf, London.

Law, J. (1994), *Organizing Modernity*, Blackwell, Oxford.

Lock, D. (2000), 'Degrees of Purgatory', *Town and Country Planning*, Vol. 69, pp. 126-130.

Lowe, P. (1977), 'Amenity and Equity: a Review of Local Environmental Pressure Groups in Britain', *Environment and Planning A*, Vol. 9, pp. 35-58.

Lowe, P., Murdoch, J. and Cox, G. (1995), 'A Civilised Retreat? Anti-urbanism, Rurality and the Making of an Anglo-centric Culture', in Healey, P. *et al.*, *Managing Cities: the New Urban Context*, Wiley, London pp. 63-82.

Macgregor, B. and Ross, A. (1995), 'Master or Servant? The Changing Role of the Development Plan in the British Planning System', *Town Planning Review*, Vol. 66, pp. 41-59.

Marks, G. (1996), 'An Actor-centred Approach to Multi-level Governance', *Regional and Federal Studies*, Vol. 6, pp. 20-40.

Marsden, T., Murdoch, J., Lowe, P., Munton, R. and Flynn, A. (1993), *Constructing the Countryside*, UCL Press, London.

Marsh, D. and Smith, M. (2000), 'Understanding Policy Networks: Towards a Dialectical Approach', *Political Studies*, Vol. 48, pp. 4-21.

Mason, D. (1999), *Environmental Democracy*, Routledge, London.

Matless, D. (1995), *Landscape and Englishness*, Reaktion, London.

Mazza, L. (1995), 'Technical Knowledge, Practical Reason and the Planner's Responsibility', *Town Planning Review*, Vol. 66, pp. 389-409.

McNay, L. (1994), *Foucault: a Critical Introduction*, Polity, London.

Miller, P. (1990), 'On the interrlations between accounting and the state', *Accounting, Organization and Society*, Vol. 15 pp. 235-266.

Miller and Rose (1990), 'Governing Economic Life', *Economy and Society*, Vol. 19, pp. 1-31.

Mulholland and Associates (1996), 'Towns or Leafier Environments: a Survey of Family House Buying Choices', Mulholland and Associates, London.

Murdoch, J. (1995), 'Middle-class Territory? Some Remarks on the Use of Class Analysis in Rural Studies', *Environment and Planning A*, Vol. 27, pp. 1213-1230.

Murdoch, J. (2000), 'Space Against Time: Competing Rationalities in Planning for Housing', *Transactions of the Institute of British Geographers*, Vol. 25, pp. 503-519.

Murdoch, J. and Abram, S. (1998), 'Defining the Limits of Community Governance', *Journal of Rural Studies*, Vol. 14, pp. 41-50.

Murdoch, J., Abram, S. and Marsden, T. (1999), 'Modalities of Planning: a Reflection on the Persuasive Powers of the Development Plan', *Town Planning Review*, Vol. 70, pp. 191-212.

Murdoch, J., Abram, S. and Marsden, T. (2000), 'Technical Expertise and Public Participation in Planning for Housing: "Playing the Numbers Game"', in G.

Stoker (ed), *The New Politics of British Local Governance*, Macmillan, London, pp. 198-214.

Murdoch, J. and Marsden, T. (1994), *Reconstituting Rurality: Class, Community and Power in the Development Process*, UCL Press, London.

Murdoch, J. and Marsden, T. (1995), 'The Spatialization of Politics: Local and National Actor-spaces in Environmental Conflict', *Transactions of the Institute of British Geographers*, Vol. 20, pp. 368-380.

Murdoch, J. and Tewdwr-Jones, M. (1999), 'Planning and the English Regions: Conflict and Convergence Amongst the Institutions of Regional Governance', *Government and Policy*, Vol. 17, pp. 715-729.

Newby, H. (1985), *Green and Pleasant Land* [2nd Edition], Penguin, London.

North, P. (1998), 'Save our Solsbury': Anatomy of an Anti-roads Protest', *Environmental Politics*, Vol. 7, pp. 1-25.

Ouroussoff, A. (2001), 'What is an Ethnographic Study?', in D. Gellner and E. Hirsch (eds), *Inside Organizations: Anthropologists at Work*, Berg, Oxford.

Owens, S. (1994), 'Land Use and Sustainability: a Conceptual Framework and Some Dilemmas for the Planning System', *Transactions of the Institute of British Geographers*, Vol. 19, pp. 439-456.

Owens, S. (1997), 'Giants in the Path: Planning, Sustainability and Environmental Values', *Town Planning Review*, Vol. 68, pp. 293-304.

Purdue, M. (1994), 'The Impact of Section 54A', *Journal of Planning and Environmental Law*, Vol. 44, pp. 399-407.

Pratchett, L. (1999), 'New Fashions in Public Participation: Towards Greater Democracy?', *Parliamentary Affairs*, Vol. 52, pp. 241-254.

Quinn, M. (1996), 'Central Government Planning Policy', in M. Tewdwr-Jones (ed), *British Planning Policy in Transition*, UCL Press, London, pp. 16-29.

Regional Trends (1998), *Regional Trends*, The Stationary Office, London.

Report of Panel (1999), *Regional Planning Guidance for South East of England*, Government Office for the South East, Guildford.

Rhodes, R. (1997), *Understanding Governance: Policy Networks, Governance, Reflexivity and Accountability*, Open University Press, Buckingham.

Roberts, T. (1998), 'Revitalising the Statutory System', *Paper to Councillors Summer School*, Exeter.

Rose, N. (1991), 'Governing by Numbers: Figuring Out Democracy', *Accounting, Organisation and Society*, Vol. 16, pp. 673-692.

Rose, N. (1999), *Powers of Freedom*, Cambridge University Press, Cambridge.

Rose, N. and Miller, P. (1992), 'Political Power Beyond the State: Problematics of Government', *British Journal of Sociology*, Vol. 42, pp. 202-223.

Rydin, Y. (1998), 'Land Use Planning and Environmental Capacity: Reassessing the Use of Regulatory Policy Tools to Achieve Sustainable Development', *Journal of Environmental Planning and Management*, Vol. 41, pp. 749-765.

Rydin, Y. (1999), 'Public Participation in Planning', in B. Cullingworth (ed), *British Planning: 50 Years of Urban and Regional Policy*, The Athlone Press, London, pp. 84-97.

Savage, M., Barlow, J., Dickens, P. and Fielding, T. (1992), *Property, Bureaucracy and Culture: Middle-class Formation in Contemporary Britain*, Routledge, London.

Scottish Office (1998), *Land Use Planning Under a Scottish Parliament*, The Scottish Office, Edinburgh.

Scottish Office (2001), *Land Use Planning Under a Scottish Parliament: Digest of Responses*, The Scottish Office, Edinburgh.

Seldon, A. (2001), *The Blair Effect: the First Blair Government, 1997-2001*, Little Brown, London.

Selman, P. (2000), *Environmental Planning* [2nd edition], Sage, London.

Short, J., Fleming, S. and Witt, S. (1986), *House Building, Planning and Community Action*, Routledge and Kegan Paul, London.

Smith, A. (2000), 'Policy Networks and Advocacy Coalitions: Explaining Policy Change and Stability in UK Industrial Pollution Policy', *Government and Policy*, Vol. 18, pp. 95-114.

South East Regional Planning Forum (1997), *South East Regional Planning Capability Study: an Introductory Note*, South East Regional Planning Forum, London.

South East Regional Planning Forum (1998), *A Sustainable Development Strategy for the South East: Consultation Document*, South East Regional Planning Forum, London.

South East Regional Planning Forum (1999), *Regional Planning Guidance for the South East: Report of Panel: SERPLAN's Response*, SERP 540 South East Regional Planning Forum, London.

Stewart, J. (1993), 'Innovation in Democratic Practice in Local Government', *Policy and Politics*, Vol. 24, pp. 29-41.

Stoker, G. (1998a), 'Governance as Theory: Five Propositions', *International Social Science Journal*, Vol. 155, pp. 17-28.

Stoker, G. (1998b), 'Public-private Partnerships in Urban Governance', in J. Pierre (ed), *Partnerships in Urban Governance*, Macmillan, London, pp. 17-32.

Stoker, G. (ed) (2000), *The New Politics of British Local Governance*, Macmillan, London.

Tanner, R. (2001), 'Guidance for Wales Lacks Local Detail', *Planning*, April 13th, p. 11.

Tewdwr-Jones, M. (1994a), 'Policy Implications of the Plan-led System', *Journal of Environmental Planning and Law*, Vol. 46, pp. 584-593.

Tewdwr-Jones, M. (1994b), 'The Development Plan in Policy Implementation', *Government and Policy*, Vol. 12, pp. 145-163.

Tewdwr-Jones, M. (1995), 'Development Control and the Legitimacy of Planning Decisions', *Town Planning Review*, Vol. 66, pp. 163-181.

Tewdwr-Jones, M. (ed) (1996), *British Planning Policy in Transition*, UCL Press, London.

Tewdwr-Jones, M. (1997), 'Plans, Policies and Intergovernmental Relations: Assessing the Role of National Planning Guidance in England and Wales', *Urban Studies*, Vol. 34, pp. 141-162.

Tewdwr-Jones, M. (1998), 'Planning Modernized?', *Journal of Environmental Planning and Law*, Vol. 50, pp. 519-529.

Tewdwr-Jones, M. and Allmendinger, P. (1998), 'Deconstructing Communicative Rationality: A Critique of Habermasian Collaborative Planning', *Environment and Planning A*, Vol. 30, pp. 1975-1989.

Thomas, H. (1996), 'Public Participation in Planning', in M. Tewdwr-Jones (ed) (1996), *British Planning Policy in Transition*, UCL Press, London, pp. 105-118.

Thornley, A. (1993), *Urban Planning Under Thatcherism* [2nd Edition], Routledge, London.

Urban Task Force (1999), *Towards Urban Renaissance*, Department of Environment, Transport and the Regions, London.

Vigar, G., Healey, P., Hull, A. and Davoudi, S. (2000), *Planning, Governance and Spatial Strategy in Britain: an Institutionalist Approach*, Macmillan, London.

Wall, D. (1999), *Earth First! and the Anti-roads Movement*, Routledge, London.

Warburton, D. (1998), *Community and Sustainable Development*, Earthscan, London.

Warburton, D. (2001), 'Participation in the Future', *Town and Country Planning*, May, pp. 148-149.

Ward, (1994) *Planning and Urban Change*, Paul Chapman Publishing, London.

Wenban-Smith, A. (1998), *Memorandum to Select Committee on Environment, Transport and the Regions Tenth Report: Housing*, The Stationary Office, London.

World Commission on Environment and Development (1987), *Our Common Future*, Oxford University Press, Oxford.

Young, S. (2000), 'Particpation Strategies and Environmental Politics: Local Agenda 21', in G. Stoker (ed), *Power and Participation: the New Politics of Local Governance*, Macmillan, London, pp. 182-197.

Index

Acts of Parliament *see* statutes
Adam Smith Institute, on the planning
  system 19
Aylesbury
  housing proposals 116
  market square, photo 113
  population growth 89, 93, 102, 112,
    116
Aylesbury Vale
  description 112
  District Local Plan 113-18
  housing proposals 114, 117-18

Bell, Graeme 78
Blair governments (1997-), and the
  planning system 30
brownfield sites
  Haddenham village 126-9
  and housing development 138
Brundtland Report (1987), and
  sustainable development 28
Buckinghamshire
  Chilterns AONB 94, 95, 96, 98
  County Hall, Aylesbury, photo 90
  County Structure Plan
    Baseline Strategy 94, 95
    and the CPRE 104-5
    development restrictions 93-4
    district input 95
    EiP 99-107
    and the HBF 101, 102, 103
    map 85
    public consultation 96-8
  Green Belt 94, 95, 96, 97, 98
  household projections 102, 103
  housing demand 97-8
  population growth 89-90
  and sustainable development 95, 98,
    106, 129
  see also Aylesbury; Aylesbury Vale;
    Haddenham village
Burton, Tony 80

census data, use in housing forecasts 67-8

Chelmer model, housing forecasts 103
Chilterns AONB, Buckinghamshire 94,
  95, 96, 98
coalitions, and governance 6-7
conservation, and planning 3-4
Consortium Developments Ltd, housing
  projects 23
counterurbanization
  origins 34-5
  and pastoralism 37
  and planning 38
  and politics 38
  reasons for 37, 88-9
  see also population changes
counties
  and development plans 55
  and housing forecasts 70-1
  population changes 35
  and structure plans 55
Country Life, on development 38-9
Countryside Alliance 73
Countryside Marches 40
CPRE (Council for the Protection of
  Rural England) 3, 70, 78
  and Buckinghamshire County
    Structure Plan 103-6
  on housing forecasts 72, 138-9
Cullingworth, Barry, on the planning
  system 26

DETR (Department of the Environment,
  Transport and the Regions)
  Planning Inspectorate 45
  publications
    *Guidance on Preparing Regional
      Sustainable Frameworks* (2000)
      54
    *Modern Local Government: In
      Touch With the People* (1998) 58
    Modernizing Planning (1998) 49
    *Planning for the Communities of
      the Future* (1998) 73, 74, 77
  role in planning system 45
development

Buckinghamshire, restrictions 92-3
Country Life on 38-9
and planning policy 3
see also sustainable development
development plans
    complexity, increase in 57
    and counties 55
    and local discretion 59-60
    and Planning and Compensation Act
        (1991) 59-60
    and planning policy 55
    and PPG notes 45-6, 47-9, 59, 62
    and public participation 33-4
    purpose 20
    significance 43-4
    The Future of Development Plans
        (1986) 20
developmentalism, and
    environmentalism 3, 111, 133-4, 146-7
district councils, and the planning system
    19
DLP (District Local Plan)
    Aylesbury Vale 113-18
    and structure plans 114-15, 129

earnings, south-east region 87
economic development, and planning 21
economic sectors, south-east region,
    table 86
EiP (Examination-in-Public) panel
    Buckinghamshire County Structure
        Plan 99-107
    criticism of SERPLAN 77
Environment Secretaries
    Chris Patten 23-4, 27, 28
    John Gummer 27
    John Prescott 27, 40, 58, 73
    Michael Heseltine 18
    Nicholas Ridley 23
environmentalism, and
    developmentalism 3, 111, 133-4, 146-7
ethnographic study, Haddenham village
    5
Euro-elections, Green Party 23

Foxley Wood, housing development 23
France, population density 1
Future of Regional Planning Guidance
    52

General Development Orders 45

governance
    and coalitions 7
    and government, comparison 6
    and governmentality, comparison 10,
        135-6, 145
    meaning 6
    and planning 45
    and planning theory 7-8, 10
    and policy making 6-7, 43
government, central
    and planning policy 45-9, 65-6
    and regions 142
    and governance, comparison 6
    and statistics 11
governmentality
    and governance, comparison 10, 135-
        6, 145
    meaning 8-10, 136
Green Belt, Buckinghamshire 94, 95, 96,
    97, 98
Green Party, Euro-elections 23
Gummer, John, Environment Secretary
    27

Haddenham Protection Society 121-2
    Haddenham Village Society, conflict
        127-8
    and 'NIMBYism' 126
    strategy 126-7
Haddenham village
    brownfield sites 126
    ethnographic study 5
    house prices 119
    housing proposals 118, 121, 124-5,
        128-9
    housing sites, map 123
    local plan 119-29
    origins 118
    Parish Council 128
    photo 120
    political factors 124-5
    population 118, 119
Haddenham Village Society 119-20
    Haddenham Protection Society,
        conflict 126-7
HBF (House Builders Federation) 3, 70
    and Buckinghamshire County
        Structure Plan 101, 103
Heseltine, Michael, and the planning
    system 18-19
High Wycombe, growth 93

house prices
Haddenham village 119
London 89
south-east region 87
households
Buckinghamshire 102, 103
projected growth 69
see also housing forecasts
housing
census data 67-8
new, and conflict 1-2
and planning 4-5, 66-7
planning for 5, 6, 66-7
as 'pollution' 1, 15, 38-9
projections 26-7
projects, Consortium Developments
Ltd 23
proposals, Haddenham village 118,
121, 122-4, 128-9
as 'public good' 1, 15
and regions 73-4
and sustainable development 73, 136,
140
see also housing forecasts
housing demand
Aylesbury 115, 117
Aylesbury Vale 114
Buckinghamshire 95, 97
south-east region 2, 23, 27, 75-6, 79,
139
housing development
and brownfield sites 138
and RPCs 74
housing forecasts 5, 38, 66-7, 68
Chelmer model 103
and counties 71
CPRE on 72, 138-9
and John Prescott 73
and regions 69
and SERPLAN 76-7, 80-1
and spatiality 80, 137
and statistics 12, 67-8, 71-2, 79-80
see also housing

Lifting the Burden, White Paper (1985)
20
local authorities, and the planning system
22-3, 65-6, 143
local government
and planning policy 57-9
structure 55-6

Local Government Act (1985) 20
Local Government, Planning and Land
Act (1980) 19-20
London, house prices 89

Major governments (1990-97), and the
planning system 25-7, 43
middle classes, and rural areas 90-2
Milton Keynes, growth 93, 95-6
minerals, and the planning system 65,
141
Modernizing Planning (1998) 58

'NIMBY' (Not in My Back Yard) 126,
127, 128, 136-7, 142-3

owner occupation, south-east region 87

pastoralism, and counterurbanization 37-
8
Patten, Chris, Environment Secretary 23-
4, 27, 28
planners, and planning 117
planning
and conservation 3-4
and counterurbanization 38
and economic development 21
and the environment 3
and governance 45
guidance
and RDAs 51-2, 53
regions 50-1, 53, 62-3
and housing 4-5
for housing 5, 6, 66-7
and planners 117
and politics 11
and public participation 32-4, 55
rationalities 13-15, 133-4
and spatiality 13, 139, 146-7
strategic
and RPG notes 52
south-east region 50-1
theory, and governance 7, 10
see also development plans; planning
policy; planning system
*Planning for the Communities of the
Future* (1998) 137
Planning and Compensation Act (1991)
24, 55-6, 57
and development plans 59-60
Planning Inspectorate, DETR 45

Planning magazine 48
planning policy
    approaches to 83, 139
    and central government 45-9, 65-6
    and development 3
    and development plans 56
    hierarchy 44, 62, 135
    and local government 57-8, 139
    origins 44
    and regions 49, 52, 54-5, 137-8, 139-
        40
    see also development plans; planning;
        planning system
Planning for Sustainable Development:
    Towards Better Practice (1998) 30
planning system
    Adam Smith Institute on 19
    Barry Cullingworth on 26
    and the Blair governments (1997-) 30
    continuity and change 26, 27, 30-1,
        39-40, 48
    DETR role 45
    and district councils 19
    and local authorities 22-3, 65-6, 143
    and the Major governments (1990-97)
        25-7
    and Michael Heseltine 18-19
    and minerals 65, 141
    and the private sector 19
    purpose 2-3, 39-40
    reform 144-5
    simplification 58
    speeding up 19
    and statistics 12
    and the Thatcher governments (1979-
        90) 3, 18-22, 28
    see also development plans; planning;
        planning policy
policy making, and governance 6-7, 43
politics
    and counterurbanization 38
    and planning 11
population, changes
    counties 35
    reasons for 36-7
    rural areas 35-6, 88
    south-east region 87, 88
    urban areas 36, 37
    density
        France 1
        UK 1

US 1
growth
    Aylesbury 89, 93, 102, 112, 116
    Buckinghamshire 89-90
    see also counterurbanization
PPG (Planning Policy Guidance) notes
    criticism of 46-8
    and development plans 45-6, 48-9, 59,
        62
    effectiveness 47-8
    and local discretion 59
    purpose 25, 46, 134
    and regions 74, 137-8
    see also RPG
Prescott, John, Environment Secretary
    27, 40, 58
    and housing forecasts 73
private sector, and the planning system
    19
public participation
    and development plans 33-4, 96-7
    and planning 32-4, 55
    Yvonne Rydin on 32-3

rationalities, planning 13-15, 133-4
Raynsford, Nick 138
RDA (Regional Development Agency)
    and planning guidance 51-2, 53
    purpose 51
regions
    and central government 142
    Future of Regional Planning
        Guidance 52
    and housing 73-4
    and housing forecasts 69
    planning guidance 51, 52, 62
    and planning policy 49, 52, 54-5, 137-
        8, 139-40
    and PPG notes 74, 137-8
    and sustainable development 53-4,
        74-5
Ridley, Nicholas, Environment Secretary
    23
Rio Earth Summit (1992) 29
Rogers, Richard 27
RPC (Regional Planning Conferences),
    and housing development 74
RPG (Regional Planning Guidance)
    notes
    established 50
    status 51

and strategic planning 54
see also PPG
rural areas
  attraction 89-90
  middle class character 90-1
  population changes 35-6, 88
  see also counterurbanization
Rydin, Yvonne, on public participation 32-3
SERPLAN (South East Regional Planning Forum)
  A Sustainable Strategy for the South East 77
  criticism by EiP panel 77
  and housing forecasts 76-7, 80-1
  origins 50
Skeffington Committee 32
social mobility 36-7
Soley, Clive 60
south-east region
  earnings 87
  economic sectors, table 86
  house prices 87
  housing demand 2, 23, 27, 75-6, 79, 139
  owner occupation 87
  population changes 87, 88
  strategic planning 50
  sustainable development 79, 146
  unemployment 87
spatiality
  and housing forecasts 80-1, 137
  and planning 13, 139, 146-7
statistics
  and government 11
  and housing forecasts 12, 67-8, 71-2, 79-80
  and the planning system 12
  resistence to 12
statutes
  Local Government Act (1985) 20
  Local Government, Planning and Land Act (1980) 19-20
  Planning and Compensation Act (1991) 24, 55-6, 57
  Town and Country Planning Act (1947) 32
strategic planning *see* planning, strategic

structure plans
  Buckinghamshire, case study 83-109
  and counties 55
  criticism of 20, 21
  and District Local Plans 114-15, 129
Sustainable Development: Opportunities for Change (1997) 29
Sustainable Development: the UK Strategy (1994) 29
sustainable development 3-4, 13
  Brundtland Report (1987) 28
  and Buckinghamshire 95, 98, 108, 129
  and housing 73, 136, 140
  interpretation 141
  meaning 28
  objectives 29-30
  Planning for Sustainable Development: Towards Better Practice (1998) 30
  and regions 53-4, 74-5
  scope 30-1
  south-east region 79, 146
  This Common Inheritance (1990) 28-9

TCPA (Town and Country Planning Association) 27
Thatcher governments (1979-90), and the planning system 3, 18-22, 28, 43
The Future of Development Plans, White Paper (1986) 20-1
This Common Inheritance, and sustainable development 28-9
Thornley, A., *Urban Planning under Thatcherism* 18, 24
Town and Country Planning Act (1947) 32

UK, population density 1
unemployment, south-east region 87
Unitary Development Plans 20
urban areas, population changes 36, 37
Urban Development Corporations 19-20
urban development zones 19
Urban Task Force (1999) 27
US, population density 1
Use Class Orders 45